In Praise of Th

"People today are categorised by their self-imposed branding; from the phone they use, to the shoes they wear. *The Brand Messiah* shrewdly explores this notion and challenges readers to reflect upon their own choices."

— **Geoff Burch**, *Best-selling Author & Business Expert*

"Full of intrigue, certainly one to read!"

— **Leon Bailey-Green**, *creator of brand and trend-influencers' 'Online Fashion 100' (as seen on VOGUE.COM)*

"*The Brand Messiah* is a gift of a book for people who want to understand society's 'brand-heavy' subconscious and the effect it can have on a person's everyday life."

— **Phillip Blond**, *Director of ResPublica and architect of the Big Society*

The Brand Messiah

The Brand Messiah

BY JONATHAN GABAY

Copyright © 2012 Jonathan Gabay
Cover design by Cover Kitchen Pte Ltd

Published in 2012 by Marshall Cavendish Editions
An imprint of Marshall Cavendish International

PO Box 65829
London EC1P 1NY, United Kingdom
info@marshallcavendish.co.uk
and

1 New Industrial Road, Singapore 536196
genrefsales@marshallcavendish.com
www.marshallcavendish.com/genref

Other Marshall Cavendish offices: Marshall Cavendish International (Asia) Private Limited,
1 New Industrial Road, Singapore 536196 • Marshall Cavendish Corporation, 99 White
Plains Road, Tarrytown, NY 10591 • Marshall Cavendish International (Thailand) Co
Ltd. 253 Asoke, 12th Flr, Sukhumvit 21 Road, Klongtoey Nua, Wattana, Bangkok 10110,
Thailand • Marshall Cavendish (Malaysia) Sdn Bhd, Times Subang, Lot 46, Subang Hi-Tech
Industrial Park, Batu Tiga, 40000 Shah Alam, Selangor Darul Ehsan, Malaysia

Marshall Cavendish is a trademark of Times Publishing Limited

A CIP record for this book is available from the British Library

ISBN 978 9814 328 20 3

Printed and bound by CPI Group (UK) Ltd, Croydon, CR0 4YY

**Marshall Cavendish publishes an exciting range of books
on business, management and self-development.**

If you would like to:
- Find out more about our titles
- Take advantage of our special offers
- Sign up to our e-newsletter

**Please visit our
special website at:**   **www.business-bookshop.co.uk**

For my family who give me purpose.
For my friends who give me hope.

With special recognition to Tony, Steven, Tracey
and the Midas team's touch of genius.

Thanks to Chris, Martin, Stephanie, Mike
and all at Marshall Cavendish.

PART ◆ ONE

במדבר

IN THE DESERT

Chapter 1

"I SQUEEZED A PEA amount of mint Colgate toothpaste onto my Wisdom toothbrush.

"A shot of Listerine sent shock waves around my mouth.

"I finished up in the bathroom.

"Slipped on my Gaps. Slid into my Zeus's.

"Downstairs.

"Kitchen. Bosch.

"Lactofree milk. Benecol top up.

"Nespresso coffee machine.

"Tetley, Villeroy and Bosch.

"Drove the Jag to work.

"OK, I know you know where I am going with this. So, cutting to the Tweep 140 without the full Facebook timeline drama, here's the potted highlights; no particular order – freestyle.

"Apple iPhone, Shell unleaded, Starbucks flat cap, Moleskin notebook, NatWest cashpoint, Spotify, Skype, OED online, Cannon laser printer, Bell telephone, Klipsch earphones, Montegrappa pen, Chubb lock, Samsonite case, AMEX, NCP car park.

"Oh, and of course, I would be speechless without this – the Sennheiser 5000 mike!"

The audience laughed.

Beneath a Theory black jacket, Sam wore a regular (rather than a branded) white shirt. His matching slacks were from Gap. The 'signature' pair of red Zeus sneakers, complete with retroreflection lightning bolt logos, echoed the Robert Juliat spotlights.

Sam tapped the microphone gently. Looking into the audience he smiled, held the pose and waited the prerequisite two-and-a-half second pause: the faultless rupture to light the fuse that would lead to the chumps' ultimate redemption.

One more grin. (Sincere gaze of self-reflection.) Time to reach the climax.

"You're probably sitting there thinking, 'this man is shallow'. After all, I'm an adult reciting brand names like some kid reeling off their times tables. Am I fishing for a 'well done'? What's my reward? More stuff… more trinkets…? Just to be replaced by other stuff, eventually replaced by even more things?"

"Don't tell anyone," Sam confided to the audience, "but rumour has it, the global cutback isn't just a local Greek *myth.*"

(A half-hearted finger of applause scratched the auditorium's darkness).

"You're of course right about the stuff, the recession… especially the kid. But, trust me, even when you're nine years old, times tables never make sure-fire crowd-pleasers in the playground."

"Our jobs – we business people, challengers, dreamers, chancers, star makers… is to turn 'stuff' into desires.

"Desires drive ambition. Ambition encourages dreams to be realised. If necessity is the mother of invention, then desire is the father of momentum that grows economies.

"Your businesses build brands – reputations. Your perceptiveness turns products into coveted icons for people with the right to expect quality, research, experience, safety, technology; what they can trust: authenticity.

"Brands affect every single waking aspect of our lives.

"Your work spurs creativity, ingenuity and industry. Without you, everything stops. The machine grinds down. Recessions never cease. Fallouts never stop.

"You inspire. Aspirations provide aims. Aims need effort. Effort means work. Work needs persistence. You produce: the world turns.

"You shape more than perceptions, engineer more than campaigns.

"Thanks to your bigheartedness, it's all about to add up to one massive difference."

(Confident this time of their cue, the audience applauded.)

"You turn art into practical design. The world is interconnected to over 15 billion networked devices: windows on truth and possibilities. Global internet traffic is on target to reach over 966 exabytes per year. (One EB, people, is equal to one billion gigabytes.) Data means control. Control means business. Business means numbers; the kind of exquisite figures that are just so damn munificently mean."

(A cheer rose up.)

"Where former old-world tyrants divided and dominated, new intuitive technology, sponsored and used by your wonderful organisations, listens, learns and collaborates; generating fresh springs of hope.

"I want to share with you some remarkable accomplishments achieved by the brilliant Kerry Rollins."

A beam of light shot towards the third chair in the front row. Kerry stood up.

As if James Lipton himself (from the TV series, *Inside the Actors' Studio*) had spoken, the mere mention of any name, in this case, Kerry's, sent the audience once again into rapture. A blushing Kerry sat back down. The beam faded.

"Many of you know Kerry is our VP of Global Digital Communications. She headed last year's Client, Agency, Creative, Knowledge event in London. This lady never stops: just last month, she completed the final phase of an amazing project that you are simply going to love.

"In keeping with the latest ePrivacy directive, we are going to ensure that your brand communications data remains private. Organisations that don't share your vision won't get a party invite: even if they mention Kerry's name!"

(The audience laughed.)

"One Window Aerial 9 – better known as OWA-9 – already opens on any device a single, custom-made dashboard view for all your digital promotions and products. No more 'unsubscribes' from consumers sent identical offers on different platforms; the ultimate User Experience."

(A lone "Yes!" yelped from the back of the audience. A "Woo!" from the centre made a duo of delight.)

"Sales, including those direct from Apps, are now going to automatically be processed to take into account your – frankly – spectacular donations to the new project that today is all about."

(Further sparks of approval).

High in the rigging, a 'Lampie' (lighting technician) changed the backstage spot colour filter to a profound Midnight Blue.

Sam continued.

"In July 1969 Neil Armstrong said, 'That's one small step for man, one giant leap for mankind'. Today satellites beam pictures of Earth. Out there in space, our planet shows no political borders. Knowledge has never been so readily available and accessible to all. Through technology, ideas touch every corner of Earth's global village. In every community, each man, woman and child's voice is at last being heard and heeded. Ethical brands are listening. Social brands are uniting.

"These are all reasons why I am proud to share a new control centre designed to bring us even closer: Social Media Interaction Linearization Engagement is all about deep-listening and focusing on continuous improvement. It humanises brands like never before. You can monitor 80,000 Tweets, Facebook, LinkedIn, and other social conversations simultaneously.

"Our 'scent–select–search' algorithm works in over 14 different languages. So, whether someone is looking up a new product review, checking a friend's Timeline or sharing a brand's Timeline complete with the organisation's brand back story… you'll engage seamlessly; irrespective of native platforms. Just think about it: a global PR choir spreading the news of attentive, generous brands working together – for the best. Collaboration and participation!"

Sam paused. He winced as the Robert Juliat Aledin 330LF LED light continued dishing out the chile de árbo treatment to the back of his eyes. With the main spot still drilling down on Sam, the Lampie cast a second more slender spotlight towards Kerry Rollins.

Again she stood up, this time to a Mexican wave of squeals and applause.

Kerry owed her success to being in the right place, at the right time, with the right paperwork. Her last job was Interactive Marketing VP at an IT corp. She was one of the first people to receive an MA in Social Media from Birmingham City University.

In a world of money, Kerry knew how to work her assets. A compliant attitude to management, ice-cool pulchritudinous looks and sheer verve soon got her recruited into presenting polished software clips.

The smooth e-metric demos created on Prezi and available in multiple styles, including CDFs (computerised document formats), were piped via sites like Mashable, Techcrunch, YouTube and Vimeo.

Nerds, who suffered from progressively longer episodes of Dorito Syndrome and increasing intumesence from a bad dose of twitterrhoea, aggregated the branded demos throughout the connected world.

Kerry had her elevator pitch down to a fine art. The nerds, marketers, and Excel-enterers simply drooled. So, R&B (Roberts and Barnes – Sam's agency) made her an offer. The auburn haired, Boss-suited, size 12, 28-year-old was handsomely paid. Her package included business-class travel and entertainment expenses.

In return, Kerry put together a control centre team. It offered 24/7 engagement implementation. (The service was outsourced to facilities in Holland, the Philippines and India.)

Initially the accountants suggested following the likes of Google and Facebook, who deflected a percentage of earnings via Ireland. However, despite potential public relations coverage about local employment, the control centre project wasn't big enough to justify any large-scale infrastructure investments. On the other hand, Holland, the Philippines and India offered reasonable financial incentives. Besides, the chosen countries' provincial accents were, for the most part, more than merely tolerable.

In addition to becoming a healthy profit-centre for the agency, the listening-post enabled Kerry to continue indulging her quidnunc inquisitiveness. Better still, she could go on enjoying speed-ball shots of self-esteem via Tweet, Like, Google+, LinkedIn, Digg, Stumble Upon and IM. Just as everyone could know where, who and what she was up to, so social-satchet samples of Barnes and Roberts-approved activities and client innovations were freely offered to gossip junkies at every opportunity.

Kerry also performed sales pitches at various summits and symposiums. Eager audiences of keyboard pushers and social media apologists praised her evangelical talks. She covered everything from adaptive searches to elegant social integration and digital marketing radars.

With an eye on further recognition, Kerry naively agreed to link every hypertext containing her name back to the world-respected agency. That gave Sam's people, like Alice in HR, a tight leash on the girl (just in case all the hype led her to break The Notorious B.I.G.'s 'fourth commandment').

... Back in the hall, the purrs of love softened to subdued sighs. Kerry melted into the fading limelight. As if they were proud parents, couples in the audience smiled at each other.

Wearing a griddled grin that acted as a trellis in front of his hot throbbing head, Sam joined the parents' smiles and jabbed his right index finger towards Kerry.

He continued.

"I know a lot of you will want to talk to Kerry afterwards. She'll be delivering her keynote later this afternoon. Trust me, if you want your brand to reach and touch, you won't want to miss it.

"... Virtual clouds are distributing seeds for prosperity and change. Where once content was esoteric, today it's egalitarian.

"Collectively, we are the platform upon which our children can fulfil dreams that you and I would never have even imagined."

Sam took the second of his set of three scripted pauses. Stopping abruptly, he turned from the audience.

"Bob!" he shouted at the invisible Lampie on the lighting rig. "Let everyone see each other!"

A narrow beam picked up Sam's signature red pumps featuring the glossy Zeus lightning bolt logo. Next, the beam widened to lap his body. Finally, the entire theatre was dazzled with excitement.

"Hello there!"

The audience roared.

Rubbing his eyes, before swiping his forehead, Sam stooped to pick up a small bottle of Voss mineral water from the stage floor. Walking towards the stage edge, he took a gulp. Then, as if a father sensitively advising a son just ditched by a first love, Sam spoke.

"There's a real chance here to take ideas and multiply their potential to such an extent that everyone feels a genuine sense of achievement and purpose.

"Tonight is about coalition. We've torn down walls, opened emotional brand bridges between organisations and consumers: connecting abilities with passions.

"Your brands already win respect from people you'll never meet, but whose lives are touched by your products and services – in exceptional ways.

"I am not going to stand here and kid you: the recession is real. Times are tough. But, speaking for myself, I would rather walk towards an opportunity than away from one."

(The lone "Yes!" from the back yelped again. Others from the pack, dotted throughout the audience, joined in.)

"Your graciousness is going to return the pleasure – and hope – that we *all* owe to those who gave us the privilege to be here tonight."

The third pause.

For a brief moment, Sam lost his line of thought. Feeling the burn deep in his pupils, he took another gulp of water. Unaware of his migraine, the audience were mesmerised by the drama of the moment. Glancing up at the rig once more, Sam prepared to deliver his killer line with the small, still voice that it merited.

"Bob," he said tenderly, "release the stars."

Thousands of glittering foil stars rained from the heavens onto the audience. The arena exploded into rapturous approval: snapping and whooping like a cinema of popcorn kernels.

But it wasn't over yet. As if a canny trader in Tangiers was revealing a Persian carpet, a 15 metre wide flag bloomed from the ceiling. The billowing flag featured a deep, Bora Bora-blue background. It cleverly incorporated a fish whose individual silvered scales featured one of 11 globally recognisable brand names. At the very centre of the flag, embroidered with thick golden thread were the words: *Dum Spiro, Spero: together we serve you.*

At last, putting on his Ray-Bans, Sam stood bolt-upright and motionless. To cue, the audience stood and hooted even more.

Sam bowed humbly. Recognising the visual prompt, the Lampie dimmed the lights.

Despite Sam's throbbing temple and rising nausea, judging by the response, it was a good performance. It had to be.

Chapter 2

FIRE AND BARKING; SAM could smell the smoke. The crazed barking was incessant. The heat pinched and twisted his skin into a Chinese burn.

He was trapped.

Behind and to the left, a cloak of blackness suspended by smouldering thumbs promised sanctuary from the inferno. However, Sam figured following that route, rather than looking for another plan of escape, would leave him blindly wandering even deeper into the pungent darkness.

The barking seemed to be getting closer, growing more intense. It felt as if the animal was driven to commandeer Sam's fast-withering breathing space. Ahead, he could just make out a dull red glow; the cause of all this scorching heat.

Decision time. Which way to turn?

The roasting light… or a chance stumbling through the choking smoke, and maybe into the animal's jaws?

Time was haemorrhaging. His skin crawled with demons. His head felt like a meat hook had plunged and twisted itself into it. He had to get a hold.

"Think…" he said to himself. "There must be a logical way out."

Still the smoking hands dangled the cape as if they were the instruments of a skilled matador and he was the desperately confused bull in the ring; enraged and confused by the maddened dog and swooping cape.

"Jesus, where do I turn?"

"Sammy... here."

A voice!

"Sammy!"

He strained to peer through the sooty window smothered by smoke.

"I'm coming!" he called back.

Whoever it was, they shared the same cruel chaos as he. Maybe worse.

"Where are you? Are you OK? Are you hurt? I'm coming. Don't worry!" he choked between strangled coughs.

"Sammy."

By now the barks had become so incensed that the voice was hardly audible. It evaporated into the smoke. But still Sam was determined to help. He staggered towards the palm of the Matador's dancing hands. Every step closer to the heart of the smouldering blanket squeezed his chest still tighter.

"Can you see me yet... where are you?" he spluttered.

"Sammy!"

By now, the voice was close, *really* close. But so was the dog. Its rancid breath stirred into the mist. Before long, what with the heat, and panic, it was difficult to distinguish the snarls from the voice still calling his name. Sam wondered if he had fallen into some halfway point between life and death.

A wet dribble down his leg then a sudden poker of pain. The dog's jaws sunk into his legs. It was agony. Yet, try as he did, he just couldn't scream. He was on the ground. The dog's teeth crunched down into his groin. His bladder punctured open, oozing a brown mélange of blood and urine.

The dog lapped up the pool. Sam's time had come.

Turning to face the barricade of intense heat, he accepted his fate. All he could do was wait helplessly for his eyes to shrivel like streaky breakfast bacon.

His mind was playing tricks. He felt a hand tugging at his shoulders. He assumed he was already slipping into unconsciousness.

"Sammy, baby, wake up," Jasmine cooed.

The sudden rush of sweet and sour air from the air conditioner ceremoniously blew away the stink of the dog and smoke.

Sam was back in the land of the living. He lay there. A bead of sweat tickled his eye. The embracing folds of the double bed cradled him to recovery.

"These dreams of yours… It's OK. Relax honey. Rest." Jasmine said.

Adjusting his eyes to the light, Sam winced. With one more gulp of air he was fully in Jasmine's arms. The calmer he became, the further the waves of smoke receded into a murky quagmire of memory. The only tell-tale sign left was the familiar hoarseness in his throat from early mornings and late nights.

"Quiet now," she cooed, drawing him close. Her fingers skipped through his chest hair. Each nail skimmed dexterously, pressing against his skin.

Her breath cascaded down his stomach. He felt her breasts compete with the mattress to cradle and cushion him. With each muted whistle of her breath, he felt more reassured. With her, life was uncomplicated. Simple pleasures didn't come attached with strings and responsibilities.

"Hush now."

Her lips swept any lingering angst into murky sidewalks of shadows.

As her nails brushed smoothly back and forth, a different heat simmered. With each stroke, he felt the temperature well up from the base of his spine to the tip of his tongue until, with one final judder of expectation, there was no more need to run.

The iPhone's sudden shrill cracked a seismic rupture right through the moment.

Sam reopened his eyes. He instinctively reached for the phone from the Bose DAB clock radio deck. Within seconds, he was deftly tucked back into the overcoat of skin that was Sam: dealmaker, great joke teller at breakfast briefings, keeper of secrets and realiser of dreams.

"Yup?" he whispered into the iPhone's mike.

"Hey, Sam. Morning! You were dancing. I am telling you: tap dancing!"

"Matt. It worked?"

"This is going to move things… and there's more… Where to start…"

"I love you," Sam sighed, "but do get to the point."

"'12' is in. Their PR floozies caved in."

"The actual '12'?"

"Genuinely: it's on its way!"

Jasmine stepped into a Hilton bathrobe. She began preparing the complimentary camomile tea from the precisely partitioned tray of tea bags and coffee sachets.

"Brilliant – really – totally brilliant. Thanks Matt," Sam said enthusiastically, catching those nails slice a sachet open.

"See you at the office," he continued, whilst Jasmine pulled Earl Grey's drawstrings.

"Sure, no problem Mr Bo Jangles," Matt chuckled.

Sam Roberts, the joint head of the one of the world's most successful brand communications groups, was ready.

BARNES AND ROBERTS HAD business interests in excess of three quarters of the world's countries. The group's billings accounted for over £35 billion. The income helped keep over 120,000 employees around the world from having too much spare time.

Unlike many of his contemporaries, who spent their time exclusively on answering shareholders, Sam preferred a more hands-on approach to business.

Added to his professional credentials, he was a father, husband, advisor to world-leading educational foundations, and held several low-visibility non-exec directorships on top Fortune 500 boards. When Sam looked in the mirror, despite his slim to average frame, a man with guts stared back.

He selected the contacts from his 'favourites' on the phone. A tap of his finger summoned the dialling tone.

"Hello?" the young voice answered.

"Hey you," Sam replied.

"Daddy! How did it go?"

"Good, good. You OK?" he asked his 15-year-old daughter, Mia. "Shouldn't you be at school by now? Is mum there?"

Pause (a dry 'thump' of the phone being put on a table). A sliver of shouts punctuated with stray words: "Mum... phone.... Dad..."

Eventually, the handset was airlifted from the no-man's land of ambient sound.

"Sam," Liz said in a subtly-tetchy-at-the-edges voice, "Matt rang. He said it went well. How was Frankfurt… the hotel? Did you sleep all the way through?"

"For once, I did," Sam lied. "I was totally whacked but… no damn headaches. Did the people pick up the XK?"

"Tuesday morning," Liz replied, pointing towards Mia to collect her Nuo satchel. "The man said he'd return it tonight."

"Mia OK? School fine?" asked Sam.

"Your daughter's just fine. Back soon, aren't you?" Liz asked.

"Once I've ironed out some ideas with Tom. His place is only a short walk from the Hilton. I could do with the air."

"Tell him I said to get his head out of a calculator and beard off to the barber!"

"Snip, snap," Sam joked, catching a flash of Jasmine stepping into her coat.

"Want something from duty free?" he asked, as Jasmine silently closed the door.

By the end of the conversation, Jasmine – as Gina, Claudia, and countless others drifting around the Hilton globe before her – was gone. A 50 per cent bonus on Sam's Diamond hotel loyalty card would commemorate their encounter.

WITHIN TWO MINUTES OF considering the pros and cons of refreshing the No. 19, Liz collected her keys and stepped out onto the landscaped drive of the family's Burns+Beyerl designed mansion. The distinguished family home stood some 50 miles from where Sam had just pressed the red icon on his iPhone.

Looking forward to catching up with Laura, who co-ran the boutique in the village, Liz urged Mia into the Porsche Cayenne Turbo. The car's trunk contained a green plastic carton. It held three reusable Waitrose bags, a Streamlight torch, an Ascot picnic rug, a box of work files and pens, Apple chargers, a Lucien Pellat-Finet umbrella, and three pairs of Hunter's wellington boots (two designed in classic green, and Mia's, which were coloured fuchsia). Liz shut the Cayenne's driver's door.

Sam flicked on the hotel room's wall-mounted Toshiba. The remaining seconds of a commercial from one of the agency's core sponsors were drawing to an end. The closing sequence featured the logo-fish swimming from the bottom of the screen, where the caption, *Together we serve you* appeared.

Chapter 3

A STUNNING, 25-FOOT GLASS CURVED 'welcome' reception desk dominated the ground floor of Barnes and Roberts' West End London headquarters. It was four metres in front of a wall of mirrors, some of which reflected their own reflections. Others slanted towards the open-plan reception, offering clients a different perspective of themselves – depending on whether they stood or were seated.

The reception desk featured a continuous bank of Panasonic Smart Viera television screens that leapt from one side of the furniture all the way to the other.

The 'Audio Visual Partner to the 2012 Games' displays showcased a mix of client TV commercials along with Flickr snaps of young, ambitious agency staff. Some wore damp grins just millimetres away from the lens. Others were linked as brothers and sisters in arms: a happy-go-lucky team.

A language aficionado who may have found himself in the reception area would have spotted hidden ambitions behind each Flickr smile.

Every two minutes the screens refreshed with a giant animated set of lips. Beneath the lips was the slogan: *We turn brands into kisses.*

Two svelte androgynous receptionists, Charlie and Roberta (who could easily have just stepped out of an episode of *America's*

Next Top Model) were perched like dunnocks behind the desk.

Charlie was a bronzed quisby, whilst Roberta was a brunette. Both clutched onto the one thing that gave them confidence: their looks. Seventh Sense Solutions-supplied iMacs displayed each of the receptionists' Facebook pages. At a click of a mouse, Timeline updates could be warped out of sight from any snooping eyes that somehow managed to get on the wrong side of the reception façade.

At either extreme of the reception desk sat Lalique glass bowls filled with lip-shaped candies featuring client brand logos. A handwritten card besides the bowls read: 'Please share with friends'.

Adjacent to the main reception were three elevators. Each door sported part of a large set of letters. Read altogether the doors spelt: *Where so ever you go, go with all your heart – Confucius.*

Beyond the elevators, further left of the reception, an open archway crowned with a curved, soft blue neon sign reading 'Think-Tank' led to a Café Claudius-operated bar (another agency client).

Under the ever-vigilant guard of an Austrian with a nervous tick, young Rumanian *baristas* served the brand's finest Fairtrade roasts, cakes and biscuits to agency staff. Appreciative workers included Adam Raju and Gary Browne. Adam lived in Harrow, northwest London. Gary, an Australian, came from Koongamia, Perth. He had lived in London for 18 months.

Adam's grandfather ruled a seven-strong roost that adhered to the precise time-keeping that he constantly checked against his Rolex. The grandfather's kingdom was a cramped semi-detached in an overcrowded suburban crescent. It was surrounded by other houses with their own fully-attached families and (unofficial) lodgers. The home was conveniently near two London Underground stations. Providing the train to work was caught before 7.15 a.m., seats could be found next to brand-kitted commuters who flicked through the free morning paper, or inadvertently slept on the shoulders of someone trying read the sports pages.

For the Rajus, as with the other clans in the crescent and beyond, appearances meant pride and honour in the community. Despite their combined modest incomes, and the grandfather's frugal management of the family's funds, the Rajus competed fiercely with their neighbours for status. That included parking their latest personalised, numbered, obsidian black metallic-painted Mercedes on the red-and-grey block-paved driveway. To repay car loans, whenever possible, the family caught the train to work or the bus to the local shops.

It was worth it. Big car: bigger family distinction, greater esteem and richer business reputation. Best of all were the lipstick-green smiles, belonging to aunts on flying visits from back home, where they usually drank Lipton's tea in a mug (rather than Twinings) poured from a Marmite jar-shaped teapot.

As a teenager, Adam dreamt of escaping to wide spaces with few cars, discreet privacy and the chance to be himself with whomever he wished – whenever he liked.

Gary's family lived in a detached house, complete with a detached garage. Before his international walkabout, the family home was shared with a sister and parents. The house was on a long road with few neighbours. It was conveniently near the Koongamia Oval sports ground, as well as Greenmount National Park. A second-hand Skoda Ocatvia and a Subaru Outback were parked out front. The Brownes were happy for any uncles or aunts to visit at Christmas from east coast Australia (providing the extended family fancied the five-hour flight).

As a teenager, Gary dreamt of escaping to somewhere with busy streets and unrestricted possibilities.

Adam and Gary huddled at a table in the far corner of the Think Tank.

"Ian is such a douche," whispered Adam, placing his coffee back in the saucer.

Gary pursed his lips.

"He's already let go of yet another two designers and now expects me to handle their baggage, too. I wouldn't mind, but the scuzzy client is a bloody nightmare."

"Managers are like diapers: covered in shit and all over your ass," said Gary. "Take my advice: do the minimum, claim the overtime – if it's ever mentioned – and look forward to getting ruined off your face at the weekend."

As they chatted, other staff, from copywriters to integrated digital designers, weaved their way towards tables. Arriving on safe ground and high stools, over coffees they shared hopes of writing the great adjective-filled American novel, or first interactive Hollywood blockbuster, but mostly, they just talked of getting home at a decent time.

All played a part in the chocolate dream factory. Each dreamt of great change.

"The suits don't get the meaning of creativity," continued Adam. "It's all deadlines. Everyone wants someone with extra capacity. I'm telling you, they're using the recession to fire up the unemployed welfare force."

"From employee to unemployee. Wanted to unwanted…" Gary replied, fancying himself as a copywriter.

"Witty to unwitty," Adam noted.

"Remember Eugene with the glasses who worked on the Mokave beer account? He's been unemployed for over two years now. They've got him working on some community scheme."

"Is he in trouble with the law?" asked Gary.

"No. But he might as well be. Two years is the limit. So he's scrubbing tags off walls with some ABH from Wandsworth."

"If you don't do the time, you pay the crime. I guess." Gary said.

"We might as well work in a sausage factory," Adam quipped.

"I bet, a big mystery bag," Gary teased.

A trickle of coffee accidently dribbled from Adam's mouth.

Beyond the Think Tank, with the exception of the fifteenth floor, the remainder of the reception's general décor shared the same layout as the other levels in the empire's building. White walls acted as canvasses for discreet lighting that threw out colour-coordinated puddles of shapes. (Any of which wouldn't have been out of place in a psychologist's deck of flash cards.)

The rest of the reception was sparsely furnished. A 30-foot bright red sofa was speckled with black cushions and occasional copies of Newsweek, Time, American Scientist, Wired, Mental Floss and The Economist.

More choices were available online at the Apple Newsstand. The App was accessible via one of four iPads docked in the centre of a Patricia Urquiola coffee table. One Newsstand hosted publication reported that Pope Paul VI 'clearly and prophetically denounced the dangers of an economic development conceived in liberalist terms because of its harmful consequences for world equilibrium and peace'.

GLANCING AT HIS GRAHAM watch through Ray-Bans, Sam entered the automated frosted-glass front doors. A 'hello' nod to the dunnocks received a shy smile from a bronzed young Charlie. Throwing back a suitably coquettish smile, he headed for one of the three elevators.

With a swipe of his access card, Sam pressed the blue 15th floor button and pocketed the shades. Just as the 'approaching' button was about to glow red, a second elevator opened. One of the agency's Suits stepped out.

The Suit's focus turned to a man sat on the red couch. His rum-red cheeks burnished a brandy auburn-coloured skin. He was about 50 years old. His sideburns were thicker than the hair on top. A sensible cardigan cupped his paunch. The Suit flashed the man a smile (purchased the previous weekend from a tooth-whitening bar at Brent Cross Shopping Centre).

Sam watched the bright spark behind the molars operate. Matt spoke highly of her. Amy didn't complain and was an excellent project manager. Despite a choice of many more dyed-in-the-wool (and pricey) Suits, Matt picked her to run the agency's biggest project. Matt promised her that if she could, as he trusted she would, pull it off, her salary would be on "a completely different level". Sam trusted Matt's instincts and experience and approved of the ambiguity of his promise.

Amy lived with her gifted unemployed boyfriend, Dan Izaacs. Even with his Master Certificate, sponsored by the Institute of Carpenters, work was agonisingly sparse. Seven months of watching Maury on TV announce, "You are the baby's father", underlined Dan's despondency, punctuated with moments of exclamation marks of either exasperation or enthusiasm. Add to that a rent in the wrong side of Balham, above an NHS-subsidised optician, and Dan's patience, like Maury's newly pronounced fathers, was running out.

Amy elegantly stretched out her hand to greet the middle-aged man on the couch.

Stepping into the elevator, Sam caught the tail end of the Suit's conversation. "So, really great to see you," she said to the space just above a whistle of hair on the man's scalp. "I hope you didn't have any transport problems…"

As the elevator's doors closed, a sliver of light delivered a glimpse of the man, spellbound by the Suit's backside.

Sam stepped out into a smart but unexceptional office area. It featured a single smoked-glass top desk, Brabantia wastepaper basket and two filing cabinets. A beige two-seater sofa sat next to a Myriad side table holding a Nespresso coffee machine (similar to one the back home), and a Powwow water cooler.

A large double-glazed window overlooked the street below. It revealed an endless Mexican wave of secretaries' cleavages, punctuated by commas of bald patches belonging to men who scurried awkwardly along the street towards what they hoped would turn out to be a day of semi-colons, rather than a full stop.

A small wall-mounted access keypad stood next to a closed white door.

Opposite, a 50-year old mousey-crowned woman, dressed in a smart office-grey suit, sensible shoes and electric-blue chiffon *pashmina* sat behind the smoked-glass desk. As with the reception area, the desk carried an iMac, as well as a Seimens executive phone.

The styling was very twenty-first century Noughties. Precisely Martha Reynolds: the queen of her unpresumptuous, but perfectly apportioned territory.

"Good morning Sam," greeted Martha in a clipped, cultivated GU25 postcode accent.

"Hi 'M'." (A gauche reference to the James Bond series of movies, that still amused Sam and continued to irritate Martha).

"Anything new?" Sam asked, stepping towards the white door.

"Only the regulars. Matt's pencilled in a '10.30'," Martha replied, scanning her *Economist* desk diary. "Oh, and there's that '3.30' with Ms Sanderson. I've already checked: the Konditor and Cook plate will be in time."

Making a mental note of his 'to-dos' and rather fancying a slice of K&C, Sam punched his password into the door's keypad.

"Done something with your hair? It looks great!" he called across his shoulder, as the final digit was pressed into the access panel.

"Yes!" Martha lied. "Thanks for noticing."

"For sure."

Sam stepped into the private office: his dominion of detail offering a comforting sanctuary of control.

Chapter 4

THE ROOM WAS IMPOSING. Sam liked it that way.

His Girsberger Trilax 2 office chair was tucked neatly under the Gabriel Teixido designed desk. The T-shaped classic stood in front of a set of double windows. The view offered a spectacular panorama of London that stretched far beyond the receding hairline commas and Mexican jelly-tops bobbing below.

Apart from an iMac, as with Martha's desk, the Teixido carried a Seimens telephone system.

A Carol Bimbi grey-and-white sofa (ample enough to caress six) squatted in eager expectation at the far end of the room. An SMA bookshelf stood towards its left. The silk-smooth shelves were interspersed with volumes of Phaidons, family pictures, Batman, Superman, and other comics from a bygone era, along with three delicate bonsai trees.

The rest of the room easily housed its additional 1524mm Conran coffee table, two Primo brushed steel filing cabinets (one holding a fourth bonsai tree) a wall-mounted 132.08cm flat-screen Sony, and vintage American 'Mouthy Marvin Talking' gumball machine.

For Sam, business involved making the right impression with the right people who needed to be impressed.

His father had taught him that.

Dad was Head Waiter at The Lansdowne Club in Mayfair. Each month he treated the young Sam to a flick at the Odeon in Acton. On the way, he often told the boy stories from work.

There was the one about the businessman who ordered the best of everything for his table of clients. Following a wonderful meal full of laughing and commenting on the indecisiveness of the government of the day, the man left in a Mercedes. A few weeks later, his father happened to see the same man sitting on a park bench. The man drew deep breaths of smoke from an Embassy cigarette. Despite knowing his place in the social pecking order, his father, being 'Dad', couldn't help but tentatively ask the obviously pensive man how things were?

Hesitant at first, then recognising the pleasant waiter's considerate smile, the man figured he posed no threat. Before long, for some reason to do with something that his dad said he understood, but couldn't explain to Sam, the man described how business was struggling and his endurance had been stretched to the limits.

"I hope you don't mind my asking, but what's with the club?" probed Sam's father.

"Money goes to money, rewards to people with power to bestow favours," the man replied. "People need a place to reign."

There and then, they 'clicked'. The man confided in Sam's father. Sam's father listened to the man. That chat led to a 10-year-long friendship.

In his capacity as Head Waiter, Sam's father always ensured the man had best table in the house. In return the Head Waiter received handsome tips: the man's reputation for lavish hospitality, as enjoyed by the political and business elite, became renowned.

Over the years, Sam's father arranged for an entire menu of additional extras for the man, all at no 'official' surcharge: shoe-shines, valets, hovers of waiters, champagne at the Piano Bar… He also found the man a trusted chauffer. The driver collected VIP clients from Heathrow. Each was whisked to the club, with the instructions to ask for a specific room. On the VIP's arrival, the concierge, who recognised the room's reservation, ensured that the guest was looked after.

When Sam was about 15 years old, during a weekend drive, he was telling his dad about a boy at school. Despite a reputation for bullying, annoyingly the boy was a hit with just about everyone.

That was the car journey in which Sam's father first elaborated on the craft of blowing whistles and pursing lips.

"Part of the rules of working in a big place is learning if and when to remain invisible. Let's say you believe, that despite everything, something is wrong… *think* before whistle blowing on anyone. You've got to live with your choice."

He then explained how the concierge would occasionally pop into the kitchen, downstairs at the club. The concierge once caught sight of the sous chef smuggling away a small rack of lamb to use for a family Sunday roast. On another occasion he nabbed a cleaner who had spent well over 40 minutes on the staff phone during working hours talking to her mother.

'Upstairs', following a politician's private meeting with a member of the opposition, the same concierge ensured that each party was discretely returned to their respective second homes. One was in Victoria, one in Westminster. Having both been safely despatched, the concierge personally cleared the room's coffee table of empty bottles.

"He wiped the sofa with antiseptic, and even sprayed the air with Penhaligon's cologne. Six months later the Concierge was gone. The last I heard, he was flying to a job he found at a resort in some exclusive Canadian hotel. A place called Cranbrook."

Another of Dad's stories concerned 'old bags' and 'wind'. An eminent duchess, renown for her charity work, accidentally farted in front of some distinguished guests. Sam's father, who was in the room, immediately claimed responsibility. Initially, hearing Dad's tale, Sam wasn't just shocked, but ashamed. Why embarrass himself on someone else's behalf?

"Quid pro quo, son," his father explained. "Dignity is priceless. If you can ever help someone who others really depend on – it's priceless. Add the ways and means to look after my family… well, then that same personal dignity turns into something way beyond riches."

In addition to receiving the occasional envelope containing a £50 note, in return for his fast thinking, Sam's father was slipped a telephone number. It was a direct line to a certain person, who kept more useful contacts scribbled in his Letts address book than his father could ever imagine.

Whereas during the week, Dad mastered the magic of illusions and misdirection, on free weekends he stood next to Sam, offering prayers of thanks to his supreme Father of miracles. Give or take, his prayers were mostly answered: those he served, served his purposes. What's more, he could comfortably afford little treats, including taking his son to the latest James Bond at the Odeon.

… Flicking on his 27-inch iMac, Sam reckoned that Dad had prepared him well.

SAM STIRRED A TEASPOON of low calorie sugar into the coffee prepared by 'M'. The cup's saucer sat alongside a copy of Ben Josephs'

bi-weekly R&D Trend Report. Ben was the agency's EMEA Head of Research.

Just as Sam was about to get into the report, an image of a weathered garden fence popped into his head. Sam pictured a jasmine-eyed neighbour grabbing a tantalising glimpse of a luxurious lawn on the other side of the fence. At a stretch, the irritated neighbour could see that the next fence beyond bordered an even lusher Eden. Each garden was more impressive than the last. To reach the ultimate garden, 1000 miles of fences would need to be jumped. There beyond the final hurdle, the lawn was made of Astroturf. Its realistic grass tempted sharp-eyed ravens to endlessly nose-dive into it until the concealed concrete beneath split beaks and finally snapped necks.

… Sam's screen saver was loaded. It featured a cartoon of a topless man who stood apart from a close-knit group of people all wearing T-shirts reading, 'Be you'. Unanimously, the group condemned the loner as 'non-conformist'.

Picking up Josephs' report, he began to read about the latest 'ins' that were arguably 'out', but could well end up somewhere in between the departure lounge and arrivals.

Chapter 5

SAM HAD FAITH IN Ben – at least on most things. Whilst clients depended solely on metrics and focus group reports (either of which could only reveal the past and present but never the customarily unpredictable) Sam preferred to follow the advice of his late friend, Steve Jobs: "Listen to others. Learn, but finally trust your instincts."

Their relationship went way back to the days before Tim Cook was at Apple's helm. If Sam was in town during a new Apple innovation launch, Steve usually invited him to watch a jeans-and-black-polo press briefing.

During one conference, a journalist asked what market research went into making the iPad? Sam chuckled when, without pausing, Steve replied: "People don't know what they want until you show it to them."

Following the event and late afternoon chats with Steve's inner circle, the two buddies took a 20-minute drive up the interstate 280 to an improvisation club in San Jose. The club was a testing ground for nonconformist comedians whose views were totally different than most, and yet strangely familiar to all.

The club offered hecklers two types of comics: those who stood behind an old Valan Atlas chrome microphone stand, and others who stood besides it. For the first kind of comic, if observations were a touch too blunt, or missed the sweet spot, punch lines received bloody noses.

The second variety were penned by 'middle of the night' routine writers. Their inspired scorn was scratched with stumpy branded pencils left besides motel pads. Given the right blend of 2 a.m. spite – a mellow JD whiskey and a wily smile – the self-hating bipolar comics delivered precision blows to the audience's tickle-belly hotspots, which jiggled with joy at the nut on stage who delivered gag after gag of muzzled truths.

Avoiding the subject of Steve's ever-shrinking frame (an effect of pancreatic cancer) Sam asked how 'operation i-yacht' was going?

"Perfect," replied Steve with a boyish grin. "The family's *High Society* 'True Love' get-away."

"… and friends?"

"… the perfect crew."

"How lucky we are!"

Sam mentioned the interview and the research question: "You've always had this thing about getting it just right. Hell, Apple is the world's biggest computer brand, yet you don't physically manufacture computers directly in the US!" Sam's fork just missed a wobbly cherry tomato on his plate of salad.

"I'll tell you a story. In terms of the effective production, I remember once showing engineers and executives a prototype iPhone with a scratched screen. I wanted it sorted. So they flew to China. Within six weeks they delivered scratch-free glass. Demand and supply."

Sam nodded at Steve's logic.

"Anyway," Steve continued, his voice becoming more lugubrious, "realising that I could be dead soon kind of helps me make the most important decisions in life based on what's real and true, not based on fear of failure, embarrassment, pride, or other external guesses. I don't let the shout of other people's opinions drown out my own inner voice."

"Sometimes I have doubts," Sam replied, looking at the stubborn tomato on his plate.

"Join the club. There's a Hindu proverb that kicks off a neat movie the guys in the office made for my thirtieth," smiled Steve. "The home-style movie was made of snaps from the past. (I still don't know how they got hold of them.) Anyway, the proverb in the movie's opening sequence reads: 'For the first thirty years of your life you make your habits. For the last thirty years of your life, your habits make you.'"

Steve's fork struck straight through his salad's cherry tomato. "Take it from me. Surround yourself with people you trust; ultimately follow your heart and intuition. It takes courage, but it's worth it. That's real ROI – Return On Instincts – you can't put a figure on it."

A young man on stage was finishing his routine. "Everyone says we're the home of Apple technology," quipped the comic. "They're all wrong. It's Scotland. I was over there and asked a guy if he liked his new cellular. 'Aye-phone,' he replied."

No response. The comic waited.

Still nothing. The comic slipped away. Once again, the stage was left to the only stand-up made of the right mettle to permanently glitter in the spotlight: the Valan Atlas.

Steve lifted his glass. "Stay hungry, stay foolish," he said.

"To life," Sam rejoined.

"L'chaim," Steve countered, with a twinkle in his eye.

Chapter 6

In London, Sam's most reliable people (within the 10 per cent 'C-level') regularly ran 'inner-committees' that updated other 'over-seeing' committees with progress.

One glance at Ben Josephs' report showed he was keen and talented. In addition to picking up occasional titbits from the R&D and planning group, Josephs also relied on a crop of mouse potatoes together with a fertile patch of young thinkers still naïve enough to be daring. The Spuds were paid in convention tickets and advanced software releases. The Studs were paid in party invites, art gallery openings, or whatever else their scene happened to be.

The potatoes spent their days slurping strawberry thick-shakes in cluttered offices, sole-high in comics, Bubble chocolate wrappers, cans of full-fat Coke and copies of *Wired*.

Desks stained with McIllhenny Tabasco sauce carried screens of Tweets, Bloomberg, Sky, NTD, Fox and NASA news feeds. They even had one monitor wired up to live links from a hacked satellite pointing at the enclave of America's latest bad boy on the block. Top place on their wall went to a collection of Emma Stone pictures, bordered by a tangle of spray-on spider webs.

According to Ben's report, crazes were on the move again. "Trade-up and beat-down commerce" was big with just about everyone. (In addition to driving hard bargains, the practice saw consumers trading in old products in part payment towards new models at discount prices.)

"Peeping is the new Horsemaning, replacing Owling, which is the new Planking, replacing Flash Mobbing, whose roots were in Group Mooning," the report noted.

Quirks and questions always charmed Sam. Over the years, he had dog-eared everyone from Dawkins to Franzen, Chaffey, Hawking, Frankl, Hollinghurst… and on to Beckwith, Rogers, Steinbeck, Tatz…

Books revealed thoughts. Sam couldn't help it: he was a thinker.

Sam laughed out loud at the ludicrous trends. He took another sip of coffee. Every trend's roots connected to a larger family tree, whose acorns eventually sprouted new forests of truths.

A good example was *The God Delusion*. The book reminded Sam of a classic 1929 Lucky Strikes advert. One of Ben's contacts, Anna Gibson, from the Advertising Archive, provided a copy of the ad as a term of reference for a new business pitch to a global dieting company.

'An Ancient Prejudice Has Been Removed', ran the advertisement's early twentieth century headline. The bold font stood above a hand whose cuffed sleeve read: 'American Intelligence'.

It continued:

TOASTING DID IT
Gone is that ancient prejudice against cigarettes. Progress has been made. We removed the prejudice against cigarettes when we removed from the tobacco harmful corrosive ACRIDS (pungent irritants) present in cigarettes manufactured in the old-fashioned way. Thus "TOASTING" has destroyed that ancient prejudice

against cigarette smoking by men and women. It's Toasted. No Throat Irritation – No Cough.

Smokers welcomed evidence from men in white coats. Not only were habits endorsed, but the men in white coats were amongst the era's most trusted sources of knowledge. Add a pair of spectacles and the men in white could say no wrong.

Whilst some scientists criticised Dawkins' religious autopsy, arguing that real science meant to disprove, rather approve theories, so similarly, as in the 1920s, others eulogised his research. In terms of intelligent design, the book cover in particular fascinated Sam. Dieters ruled over cravings. Existentialism exonerated existence. Man was god of kings; the cover placed Dawkins' name above all else, which was left to languish in a splodge of red.

Sam rubbed his temple. Rather than red, familiar black spots (a possible migraine) appeared. Trying to see through, or at least, past them, Sam attempted to think of something else other than owls on planks having their plumes braided by men in white coats.

Chapter 7

When Sam was at the age between sucking his thumb for comfort and biting his nails out of uncertainty he regularly joined his friends cycling bikes. They explored the local side streets, pretending that hidden alleys were airport runways, and dead end-roads rocket launch pads.

If, like all kids, back home Sam played up just a little too much, his mum would give his leg a light slap. Should that fail, she withdrew privileges, including riding his beloved Chopper bike.

Dad's approach was different. He put Sam on 'time-out'. Stuck in his bedroom, a frustrated Sam endured one of his father's talks about staying grounded. "There's always a more experienced, tougher player out there…"

Depending on his stubbornness, Sam either argued his case of injustice, or judiciously remained silent. Either way, he allowed plenty of airspace to let his father's words fly on by. By the time Dad finally left the room, Sam would have already missed an afternoon with his mates or an episode of *Voyage To The Bottom Of The Sea*.

With the coast clear, Sam usually handled the rest of the detention by getting stuck into a story. Not standard books, but way more fun comics: *Marvel* or *DC*. Even perhaps, catch up with the *Beano's* Numbskulls, who ruled the head and tickled the heart. Then, there were the Mad Fold-ins, each promising a peak into wacky insights. Finally, he could always get stuck into another Asterix adventure.

As years passed, Sam realised that Dad was right. Most people believed none was as savvy as themselves. Every social tag looked to peers who offered the string onto which they could secure their labels. Bonds included friends, family, ethnicity, faiths, business and football clubs. Collectively, the groups formed the sense of what each person felt they were, and the promise of who (or what) they could become.

Fans, cheering one another on, were not just sounding a battle trumpet to rival tribes: they were awakening their inner sense of completeness. Belief in creeds, like football fans' devotion to clubs, transcended social status.

There were the flag-waving 'fooligans' who, led by their muzzled mascots, marched to their local chippy, scowling at anyone on route posing a threat to their tattooed St. George's colours.

At the other end of the social scale, still united by football heritage, supporters included royalty. (Who were as much a part of the nation's heritage as chicken Jalfrezi or fish and chips.)

Somewhere between the centre circle and goal box, more fans still handed club pride from generation to generation. Come match day, they screamed at 'number three'. By post-match mortem beers, they moaned about finding cash for annual season tickets, followed by, "Well, I mean, you know, basically speaking – if I was manager – forget the twenty-three million, 'number three' would be relegated to the bench."

During the week, team spirits were sustained by links to club websites, Sky Sports or ESPN news. Collectively the updates revealed the progress of 'number three' (Sky Sports at home; Sky Living away).

The creed also touched talent show contestants, whose hard-luck stories, accompanied by tracks composed by a record label's long forgotten artist, won viewer votes. The viewers' confidence kept the TV channel's hotlines nicely topped up, and the producers in line for an extended series run. Most crucially, brand partnerships were struck with purveyors of everything from cheese and cardigans to eggs and socks. Deals required that the high street retailers featured the soon to be run-down runners up, in nostalgic Easter sales commercials (royalties being divvied out by the producers' management team who happened to have stakes in the record label).

One way or another, everybody scathingly held that everyone else was all 'me, me, me', whilst remaining frustrated that the real issue was, '… *but what about me?*'

Twenty-first century envy wasn't any different from timeless jealousy. The 'Me-Commerce' industry was booming. So much so that its chief narcissists could afford airline upper-deck first class seats. Squatted on chairs built to accommodate 'five course menu' sized wastes, the captains of industry were blissfully insulated from the 'what about me' coach-trippers squashed on the deck below. As the chiefs tucked away at second helpings of Cannellini bean and prune salad, the hard-pressed plebs below breathed recycled oxygen fed via discreet outlets located just under the ruling First Class's seats above.

The great chiefs of 'running bull' demanded their fare's worth from the airline. In deference, taking the £3000 a day advice of a high profile social psychology consultant, the airline's marketers ensured that each first class passenger's desk included a plastic, but opulent-looking, mini computer tablet stand. Its base was inscribed with the words, 'Pinched from our airline'.

As predicted by the psychologists, once the cabin crews' subservient boys and imperious girls were out of sight, the pocket-sized pods were pilfered. In appreciation, the vindicated psychologist received a £2000 bonus and a new client (patient) enquiry. Owing a friend in Harley Street a favour, he recommended the new client to his old friend.

Neither the bonus nor the client enquiry surprised him. The social psychology consultant had published a paper pushed on socialpsychology.org that suggested that four per cent of corporate high-flyers were clinically psychotic, concealing it through status, charisma and manipulation in the workplace.

The pycho-marketing airline tactic simultaneously delivered:

- *A flight memento for the plump pompous passenger.*
- *A score against the queens of the skies.*
- *Free publicity for the canny airline, when the 'high-flyer' showed off his seized booty to corporate shoe lickers and equally vain career slickers who dreamt of saddling up next to members of the 'Mile High Screw E'm All Club'.*

Tribes of every social genus were kept occupied in an ego space below the steely skies that loomed above their heads. Every person remained oblivious to the clear cerulean firmament, just beyond the clouds. All were convinced that they were in control (and tomorrow, it looked like it could rain again).

As a rookie ad man, Sam studied advertising greats including Packard as well as Ogilvy, who said, "Sell or else…"

Sam had business victories and losses. He ate warmed-up TV dinners in bedsits and dined at banquets in castles. Moves from one job to another were either fast-tracked, or held in the slow lane (often due to a vindictive boss with body odour or a brunette's perfume).

One rainy day, 19 years earlier, Sam had barely managed to cling onto an engagement and a short-term marriage. The engagement introduced Sam to his wealthy, well-established potential father-in-law. Despite Sam breaking up with the daughter, the potential father-in-law honoured an investment that he'd pledged for Sam's business.

As for the shortly lived marriage, vows came attached with a long-term commitment that the bride would be kept in the 'Four Weddings' style to which she had become accustomed.

The father-in-law's investments promised to return a quick profit. Thanks to a prenup, when everything fell through, the bride kept the rings and her father reclaimed his money – with interest.

It all taught Sam that circumstances changed plans: occasionally for the better, sometimes for the worse, and always testing his patience and tenacity. Invariably like fads, rather than trends, opportunities only revealed themselves briefly. Spotting, let alone capturing them, required the tracking skills of a San Bushman and the patience of a BMEX 113 train spotter.

In time, Sam settled for own rule: "Sell, or fail."

Chapter 8

Occasional screw-ups came with three options: reboot, stand up or delete.

For Sam, the first was always a good route. The victory would be delivered to all who believed in the possible against the improbable. Influence lay in the details. (Provided the details sounded appropriately detailed.)

Matt would have put it another way: "From a homeomorphic point of view, truth and sincerity are the equivalent of topological spaces with a continuous inverse function." Further, he would add, "So the mappings preserving their complete topological properties remain the same. 'Simples', as one of our competitor's clients would say."

Matt and Sam, marketing and technology: partnerships that perfected the craft of camouflaging truth with selective, but impressive minutiae, which removed the burden to cogitate.

Ever-cautious business brand owners checked with lawyers who checked facts for their clients. Others outsourced tedious detail probing to the likes of Google, Wolfram or Bing. Ignoring any sponsored ads, page links led to opinionated bloggers whose obdurate rants and reckonings were 'liked', or, following correct Twittiquette, retweeted and #FF down the line.

Former professionals became skilled bloggers. Commentaries

provided white sticks for the blight-blinded jobless and life-seeking employed. Despite smuggling occasional twagarisms into their rants, bloggers were either abhorred or adored by converts or couriers.

In the race for credibility, prolific output promoted the bloggers to become local radio-talk jocks. As audiences grew, listeners/Tweeters, comprised mostly of embittered lemon suckers, tuned in.

The people's popular phone-in whines attracted more sponsorship money. (In one case, including a news bulletin deal with a grocery chain, selling bargains at 'nutty-prices'.) Some bloggers graduated further still. Their names were added to a rent-a-quote (RAQ) database of recognised professionals and/or dogmatic commentators.

RAQs helped media researchers, producers and editors fill the yawning gap in broadcasting schedules. Editorial judgement to feature opinions was based on factors including:

- *Availability, if a more renowned RAQ with broader on and offline recognition couldn't be found.*
- *Fee.*
- *RAQ's fan base reach and suitability.*
- *Sombreness/concern/disdain for a specific news issue.*
- *The RAQ's recognised experience, either practice-based and/or academic.*

However, if any experts came across as particularly authoritative, witty or exceptionally cocksure, then, irrespective of celebrity status or fees, that RAQ trumped all others.

Rent-a-quotes were great mood levellers: far more powerful than any prescribed downers. Watching them made the lemon suckers wince with even greater disdain over the sour state of crime/

youth/banks/wages/society/politics/economy/religion/business/ immigrants...

Whilst some bloggers' prophesies of doom turned out to be profitable career moves, the bloggers themselves could only ever remain as envoys of the ultimate measures of accepted truth. This was the cluster of universally acclaimed technologies (such as the one Sam evangelised about at the Brand Fish gig).

Trust was ranked by how many people relayed an expert's baton of opinions. If enough traffic was despatched via a particular courier (often adding his or her own twist to a view), eventually that person could receive the accolade of being named a 'key influencer' by social media savvy marketers. Beyond that, one day they may even become a respected RAQ.

Before long, an entire industry sprung up of torch bearing, steady-handed brand name marathon runners. Similar to adverts that featured opinion polls supporting everything from cat food to hair products, depth of truth was given credence simply by how many accepted, without question, the courier's reliability. The untied taciturnity of none became louder than the voice of one. Or as the adverts would put it: "Nine out of ten people can't be wrong".

In keeping with Kerry's project, the WWW was probed by MMM software which mixed, mangled, munched and spat out CTRs (click thru rates), CTAs (cost per acquisition), CPMs (cost per 1000 impressions)... along with an entire index of acronyms to out-step any unexpected Google dancing.

Branded YouTube or Vimeo shorts typically featured a social community and analytics VP or, better still, an obscure academic. Voiced-over animated infographics extrapolated plausible reasons to invest in the latest all-singing metrics software.

Make numbers big, and the effort to figure them out small, and you're onto a winner, thought Sam.

According to an Apple store 'genius' wearing an official T, Sam's iMac had a screen resolution of 2560x1440 pixels, 16GB 1333MHz DDR3 SDRAM, but a small footprint.

"Awesome dude," Sam remembered the geek squeal with delight.

Chapter 9

THE THIRD SUBJECT BOX down the 27" screen was from Peter. He was a competitive Suit who stalked the same floor as Amy. (Under his breath, Peter often cussed Amy for landing sports and leisure accounts whilst he was stuck with razors and rechargeables).

The Outlook read: 'Philington: numbers Q2'.

The Phillington project involved the creative teams developing a campaign promoting a vacuum stubble and beard trimmer. Research concluded that the product intimated the need for a message about natural ruggedness. Trying not to go too much into Comic Sans talk, a UI (user interface) designer suggested that the trimmer inferred 'independence in a conformative world.'

At the time, Sam questioned the now all too conventional 'don't conform' creative approach. (The technique was usually tucked away in the box called 'works every time' alongside with 'shut out the world, stay in your own bubble'. The Pandora's box of well-worn ideas were preserved for clients like car manufacturers left with the Hobson's choice of promoting one model without compromising another in its fleet.)

Peter assured him there was still mileage left in the ploy. The team settled for a variation that featured a street-wise poster campaign featuring a QR code link to a short (Edward) Bear Grylls video invite. The posters were backed up with a Facebook 'Fan' site featuring more competition details to join Bear Grylls on an adventurous trip to the back of nowhere.

The 'tough-guy' adventurer promised to teach a lucky city dweller how to swallow any passing opportunity ('protein breaks') without throwing up. (It was all too easy to step on or pass by breaks included the odd scorpion, silkworm pupae, or witchetty grub.)

However abhorrent the prospect of crunching a squirming insect, let alone licking sticky lips long after the insect's exoskeleton was swallowed (its thick puss still trickling down the throat), the prize was worth it for a man of grit with a grizzly face. (Even if the Grizzly's only long-term reward turned out to be dining off tales describing the 'chickeny' taste of a witchetty grub to impressed friends down the pub.)

The team instructed Sarel Jansen, one of the most inventive photographers in the business, to capture the face of the rugged metrosexual man-scout.

Billboards featuring the peach-fuzz champ standing in a concrete jungle were erected in city centres throughout the country. The headline: **DON'T BE THE ARROW, PULL THE BOW** asserted itself in Helvetica bold. Towards the bottom of each poster an invitation was given to visit the official Facebook competition page.

The result: a 38 per cent sales increase over three months, a fit click-through rate for the Facebook page, and enough pocket money for Edward G and pals to enjoy 10 days of pampering at Richard Branson's Necker Island. (Not forgetting, as detailed in Peter's email, a tidy profit for the agency.)

Chapter 10

LONG BEFORE MAY 8TH, 1886, when the Jacob's Pharmacy in Atlanta first sold Coca-Cola, as today, every company essentially had two brands: the public brand, and the internal brand. The internal brand was aimed at the cogs, which kept the machine moving: employees, suppliers, partners, shareholders… If the internal brand was happy, like a beetroot stain, goodwill permeated every surface throughout its public-facing marque. It was just one reason why Sam believed his 'it's all in the details' school of thought worked so well. The general workforce accepted most assertions when supported by a pie-graph graphic or pregnant line diagram.

The old GE bell curve model was one of many principles that influenced Sam's thinking. He first read about the model ages ago when, as a rookie he took his first dips into possibilities.

Twenty-five years earlier, Sam sat in a 61x122cm toilet cubicle reading a pocket sized '101' management manual. The cubicle squatted in between two other boxes. The smell of ammonia and waft of sugared hot doughnuts, freshly made at a nearby coffee shop, permeated the gents. The coffee shop was the launch pad for Road Warriors like Sam, who courageously pointed their cars towards the Interstate 90, stretching 4.98735 km from no point to a great hope.

The 101's author was weaned on the old ABC ('Always Be

Closing') rule of selling. Caffeine, a packet of Winstons, willpower and pure dread fuelled his resilience. Each locked sales opportunity still opened a small, but important lesson that the author scratched out in a small, Wal-Mart purchased notebook. Those notes led to questions, which led to libraries, that steered him to more books read over a hot coffee and 'All-American Slam' dished up at Denny's. (The same Denny's which, coincidently decades later, Sam would stop at for a Mac 'n' cheese with coffee and App download.)

Eventually the author turned out a successful series of pithy pointers in sales and management. The 120-page caricature-illustrated instruction manuals paved the author's route to conference halls packed with new generations of road-battling 'consultants'.

Rather than carrying sales journals, the consultants gun-toted mobile EPOS terminals. If targets were missed, sales failure became a "deferred success". Some things, however, never changed. Too many "deferred successes" still ended up in "discontinued working relationships".

Before finally claiming an 'Early Bird' discount ticket for the conferences, consultants tried everything from booze, screws, NLP and SPIN... to popping the odd 'E': anything to dispel and displace the same dread-end sale that the author originally experienced.

Standing on stage, next to an easel, with pad and three Sharpies, the author rattled off standard 'door-in-the-face' and 'decision fatigue' principles. Either usually satisfied most of the audience. His final fail-safe advice: another Winston and steaming cup of coffee sweetened with heaps full of courage, pleased all.

A succession of conference gigs, DVDs and CDs paid for his divorces. They also covered vast hotel suites whose many all-inclusive features covered everything from a walk-in massage shower unit to upgraded TV dinner, complete with cutlery wrapped in a napkin.

In time, an intercontinental media and publishing giant bought the author out for US$85 million. The publisher had partnered with some of the world's most exalted educational institutions. The alliances gave the publishing giant in-roads to grabbing IP from endorsed names that worked for the accredited institution (now, indirectly, the publishing giant). In return, the institutions received global distribution of their academic work. The names became spotted, and the giant cast an even bigger shadow over any enterprising upstarts.

By the time Sam was running Barnes and Roberts, the '101' manuals had become downloads, then online communities and Apps. As for the author, the deal ensured his kids entered the best universities.

The author's parents could never have afforded such an education. Mom was a diligent Daytons shop girl who respectfully attended to a customer's enquiries. Dad was a news kiosk hawker who yelled out headlines and caught up on journal reading.

Back in 1955, magazines available from his kiosk included *Christianity and Crisis*. A best-selling issue mourned the pressure on Americans to "consume, consume and consume, whether we need or even desire the products almost forced upon us".

Each night, come the last copy sold of the 'late night extras', he made his way home, whistling the catchy tune, "I like bananas, because they have no bones" – a classic tune adopted by a grocery chain as a radio jingle to promote their 'fruity prices'.

The original 101 manuals recognised that without structure, like poor countries ruled by corrupt leaders, corporate organisations would achieve little. As with countries lacking the appropriate social infrastructure to operate and grow, so corporations required employees to work as one, reporting to some, who reported to a few, who mostly answered to one.

The author recommended that the top performing 20 per cent of employees should be rewarded with offers and stock options. Like cultivating mushrooms, the 80 per cent were to be kept in the dark.

Sam's new world economy fine-tuned the formula. He knew that the entire chain was only as strong as its weakest link. The prototype 20 per cent were levelled out to no more than 10 per cent. As for the rest, tactics to keep them moving included (whenever possible) using contractors, occasionally rewarding industriousness with treats, and general contract insecurity rather than unswerving certainty. Such strategies meant the agency could even save on pensions or redundancies.

Chapter 11

THE WORKFORCE'S 90 PER cent knew their place and played their role. Each depended on the other to share the dead weight of over-loaded schedules and undermining managers. All fought threats to precious annual summer holidays on beaches, where refugees sold pigskin bracelets from suitcases and locals served leathery kebabs.

In the never-ending scuffle to preen the body of their host, the 90 per cent rarely questioned the upper 10 per cent, whose whims and quirks could make or break livelihoods. The more powerful 10 per cent were bonus-hardened. Jobs paid for home comforts which they would never have time to share, but at least perks offered consolation for making daily sacrifices to their own bosses – who stood above everyone else.

This Titanic dynasty of bosses were on first name terms: Sam, Mark, Rob, Warren, Philip, Rupert, Bernard, Tim… all being the least trusted by the other. In America alone, Titans belonging to the richest one per cent of the population held 43 per cent of the nation's wealth. All Titans occupied innermost chambers tucked within the uppermost echelons of the influential minority.

Even if meddlers (usually the press or agitated personalities) maliciously ousted management practices as 'abuses', the deferential 90 per cent stood by the Titans. After all, the 90 per cent were assured that their betrayed Caesar must have been unaware of the duplicitous management 'Liberators' (led by a modern-day Gaius Cassius Longinus or Marcus Junius Brutus).

Providing Caesar could also convince the censors (the company's shareholders) that, despite rumours to the contrary, their interests were in fact prudently managed, he could survive another year.

For all employees there was honour to be earned from an honest day's living. For Sam, there was grace in work.

Teams in unobtrusive, open offices in unexceptional cities typed messages to each other via soundless keyboards on prefabricated desks. Working *with,* rather that *at* the 'guys', departmental managers monitored it all from window-walled booths, which incorporated quick-closing vertical blinds.

At advertising agencies from Chicago to Glasgow, the upper 10 per cents joined pods of Meeting Whores who delineated and dissected the insight of an insight (or as one recently described it: "the pealing away of the onion to explore cognitive extrospection").

Empty suits made space in their packed schedules to 'just have a quick word' with unpaid Parsons or Oxbridge graduate work placement saps about questionable colour choices in the division's slide stacks.

Sales professionals set the harshest goals. Each charmer had an eye on progress charts, kept cards close to the chest, and one finger on a LinkedIn that could lead to better commissions or firmer ground.

Everyone watched his or her step. Thanks to blue-eyed Cassandras, whose auto-cued news was read and broadcast to corporate receptions, all remained uncertain of job security. The stream of bulletins (broken only by branded messages of quality and style for the bright and cool) questioned the motives of personalities, police, civil servants, tycoons, poor, rich, ordained, NEETs (Not in Education, Employment or Training), homeless, middle class… an infinite smorgasbord of tasty news-bites, filled with layers of incredulity, which kept the public constantly on their mettle.

Those able to afford the annually hiked-up commuting fares were shunted to office entrances. Vedettes perched on soiled high chairs guarded the vacuous receptions. The optical turnstile sentries dipped their heads to each passing outline that floated through and then into an inner hall where projectors cast open a gigantic window to Sky's latest blonde-shell warning.

Despite struggles to avoid those piercing blue-eyes, some mornings rice-cracker slim secretaries called Daphne, or podgy salt and vinegar accountants named Alan… or an endless train of other passport pictures heat-sealed on numbered ID cards, simply couldn't help but glance over their shoulders (as heaps of Lot's wives had done before).

The ones who made it ended up squashed into a corner inside an Otis elevator. Along with the rest of the lab rabbits caught in the headlights, they stared at the LED level indicator doing the digital tango. Some pulled themselves away to sneak a peek at a magisterial manager who twiddled with his D&Gs, S&M style (*squinting* eyes and *moving* specs up the bridge of his or her nose). A sure sign that sprinkled salt over any rabbit's sweet hopes for a torture-free day.

The listless who fell off career paths to take long-term gardening leave or grab short term hope of finding a better job became chums with friendly local chemists. As the shop's muzak system played the Muppets' 'Life's a Happy Song', the career comatosed stared idly at shelves of Ultra-Thin condoms and bottles of mouthwash. Meanwhile the whistling pharmacist crosschecked a computer, before merrily dispensing monthly mgs of anti-depressants.

The pharmacists' jars of oval-, round- and diamond-shaped

coloured pills, with appropriately scientifically sounding brand names ending with *–on*, *–ac*, *–oft*, *–am*, *–in* and *–yl*, were recommended to cost-conscious GPs by pharmacological consultants. The sales rep's express elevator pitch included leaving the good doctors with a branded, nodding bobble-head doll – the perfect companion to share the day's 10 minute allocated slots of sensitivity and understanding.

Popping a migraine pill, Sam finally closed Ben's report.

Chapter 12

WEARING NOT SO MUCH as a grin on her face as a glint in her eyes, Alice Larson, Sam's Director of Talent (HR), sat in her eighth-floor office. It was just 17 steps from one of the building's three Otis elevators.

Alice's office was decorated with pictures of idyllic landscapes from a bygone era of some place not many had ever seen. She had always been smart. (That's why, as with Amy, Sam hired her.)

Her King's College degrees in psychotherapy and psychology opened the doors to a youthfully raw but well intended attempt to heal the discouraged and disorientated.

By the time she reached the age of 37, Alice realised that her life's soundtrack was beginning to sound like the ballad of Alice (Lucy) Larson (Jordan): each year robbed her of another chance to ride through Paris in a sports car with the wind in her hair.

Her £39k NHS salary would never compensate playing the role of a Sancho Panza-esque echo chamber to 'client' calls for help. Successions of contorted faces belonging to secluded shells shat their remaining dignity onto plastic chairs at grotty clinics.

A soaked Mental Health services had grown exhausted and despondent by the interminable sounds of people's lives being flushed away. The 'Big Society' was just too big to remain a caring community.

Time, Alice had thought, to pull out from being a 'melancolonic hydrotherapist', and join what the 'empty seats' would denounce as 'the enemy'.

The £80k plus bonuses at Barnes and Roberts was hers for the taking. The offer came by way of connections provided by her former left-wing dreamboat lecturer. Enchanting young women and sanguine would-be social redeemers attended his psychotherapy class. The charming lecturer explained how his career started 'in the deep end' as a prison counsellor to the criminally insane.

He had spent the five years of his career banged-up for stretches of an hour at a time in various cells trying to reason with manipulating, self-pitying passive/aggressive men whose victims had been on the receiving end of either gentle words, cutting comments or slashed faces.

His training prepared him well. Today, when not trying to second guess which possible delusional disorder a passing stranger could be suffering from, the Bsc. (Hons) Psychology charmer specialised in reasoning with entrepreneurs, barristers and dentists (who increasingly suffered from dysthymia). He worked from a smart room in Harley Street, overlooking a green plaque that commemorated Lionel Logue's stuttering calling that turned into an eloquent career.

Networking led Alice to place several perspicuous posts on LinkedIn groups including the Consumer Insights Group, Psychology in Business Group and Society for Human Resource Management.

She devised a 'progressive' approach to institutionalised self-mortification. Her Five Star (double A, triple S) Talent System was loosely (very loosely) based on the classic work of Erving Goffman. The approach took into account what her blogs referred to as, "The organisation's talent ecosystem resonating with employees enterprise-wide". She elaborated: "This involves delivering tailored internal brand values, and most of all, corporate consideration for the individual. By caring, we create ambassadors, who promote talent sustainability. These are leaders that encourage leadership, under the original leader's discretion and direction."

Alice combined technology with cost effective 'hominian tactility'. This, for example, included subsidised massage, Yoga and Reiki sessions (all available after hours, or during lunchtimes).

Intranets provided employees with the chance "to contribute". However, whilst most happily revealed their deepest passions and latest stained blouses on Facebook, when it came to the ISB (Intranet Suggestion Box) few dared to publish honest views. Most submissions were links to articles chosen to add another layer of professional make-up to an employee's credentials.

Before long, #HR tag chasers picked up her take on 'Frame Analysis' and 'hominian tactility', along with 'presentation of self', 'intrinsic and extrinsic motivation' – all with a splash of customisable intranet dash-boarding thrown in for good measure.

The HR zealots and talent advisors mixed with techies, who encouraged decision makers, who in turn recalled her name mentioned at a weekly emotional blood-letting session with their top man in Harley Street.

Eventually the whole shebang convinced Sam to continue investing in her talent strategy. As he saw it, the 'double-A, triple-S' Star System meant:

* *Anchoring of training packages to close capacity gaps.*
* *Appropriate workforce motivation.*
* *Scoping for future recruitment needs.*
* *Segmentation of employees and occupational sets.*
* *Skills surplus or shortage study.*

… Fitted nicely besides his Bell model. It delivered a strong ROI.

'Star One' integrated highly lauded, low-cost People Awards. The associated pomp and PR drew sponsorship from the agency's clients, who also looked to enhance their own teams' 'talent sustainability'.

The awards spun into joint client/agency training mornings. Representatives of each party, either client or agency, were updated on new processes, such as improved digital and traditional brand guidelines as well as social media netiquette. One supermarket client required every sheet of headed paper (not follow-on sheets) to feature a 1pt line on the top left hand corner, printed in either PMS 109 (web: #f9d616), PMS 1235 (web: #fcb514), PMS 2738 (web: #2d008e) or PMS 362 (web: #339e35). The trainees were told that the printed lines represented the brand's originality and diversity.

There were training sessions explaining which buttons to press for software that handled everything from traffic and scheduling, to digital asset management, online monitoring and media analytics.

Providing a speaker's talks featured expressions like 'robust', 'traction', 'drag and drop', 'paradigm', 'UI', 'simplify', 'cross-platform', 'reciprocity', 'social sharing', 'accountable' and, of course, 'fully integrated future-proofing', the trainees were happy (either because the steady flow of words reassured, or tranquilised them during the well-deserved morning break).

Most speakers were pre-approved by Kerry Rollins. She always kept a Moleskin in her pocket (just in case a killer buzzword for a future presentation was on the lose).

Occasionally, in addition to free training provided by clients or wannabe 120 day payment terms suppliers, the waddling 90 per cent were also fed 'officially endorsed', externally-led training days from headless Bodies with appropriate HR-approved credentials.

Certified workshops were marketed so that higher-priced days implied more practically experienced trainers. But most of the time, cheap but charming marketing 'Medicine Men' PowerPoint Bunnies or laid-off managers lead the short-term fix programmes.

Underpaid college lecturers with too much spare time on their hands and not enough cash in their pockets gladly accepted the opportunity to repeat scripted content day-in and day-out (with breaks during business holiday seasons).

Attendees returned to their office chairs with Continued Professional Development Points credited to their annual membership pre-paid accounts. Hewlett Packard printed certificates provided space for their name, a pre-printed signature of the trainer's name, as well as the official trade association logo. The certification was added to CVs, alongside listed hobbies such as 'participating in sports', 'volunteering', 'traveling', 'reading', 'going out to eat', and 'social browsing'.

'Star One' training days tackled a perennial PR problem: employees always remembered what you did to them, rather than for them. HR was heralded for mapping career training against professional sales standards. Clients gained useful deflective PR – especially if an in-coming CEO was set to announce further rightsizing.

As for the approved training suppliers, contracts covered overheads and 'donations' to their sponsored publishing giant. More importantly, they paved the way to persuade government-training inspectors that procedures followed best-practice standards.

Once the supplier's annual official accreditation was renewed, a further year of work from best-practice HR marionettes could be guaranteed.

Chapter 13

IN ADDITION TO THE training, Think Tank café, free Red Bull
Editions and biscuits on each floor, selected 10 per cent managers
had budgets for Christmas client dinners, and were offered tickets to
industry business briefings.

Global conferences sat them at tables next to potential clients and
pestilential contenders. Depending on a client's sophistication and
manager's expenses, the Suits plied clients or contenders with drinks
and smokes. Some offered Martell Cordon Bleu and draws on La Flor
Dominicana Double Ligero cigars, but for most, cheap white wine
and vodka mixes invariably spilt the beans (and exterior sphincter).

Everybody, with the exception of workers on the first and
second floors, appreciated the summer tri-weekly Friday reception
concerts, performed by talented musicians. Unpaid performers
hoped to be spotted by the trendiest creative people in the business.
Staff contributions towards the charity concerts were donated to
NABs (the National Advertising Benevolent Society), which offered
career guidance and financial support.

Outside the reception windows, passing art bums watched the
performances, and dreamt of one day having an unpaid internship at
the coolest agency in town.

Christmas corporate get-togethers were standard annual morale boosters. There were two tiers of get-togethers. The upper echelon was reserved for top clients, their partners, and senior 10 per cent C-levels. Chandelier-crowned venues accommodated the formal events.

During such comfort breaks, excess Pavillac was leaked in between visits to Moulton Brown-supplied rest rooms. During rest periods, the fruit was dribbled out with a satisfying long finish.

Ballotines of partridge, smoked duck and Savoy cabbage insulated with date purée were gulped down, along with conversations about the "sheer hell" a client's PA went through to get planning permission for one of the outhouses to be restored. (Its blueprint inspired by *the* "always wonderful" *Grand Designs* TV show.)

On one such Christmas, simply by being in the wrong place at the right time, Matt saved a valuable client account from being terminally lost.

The client, a property developer with recurring back pain, stood a feisty 5 foot 6 inches tall. In his spare time, he practiced *Jeet Kune Do*, a martial art designed by Bruce Lee, and the cause of his backache. The developer had negotiated a tidy incentive from the Mayor of London's office to build an impressive office tower for the Olympics. The building was to be self-heated, recycling it's own waste warmth. The glass tower promised outstanding views of Tower Bridge for honoured guests to watch the GE and EDF lit, *son et lumièr* Olympic ring displays. (An initiative part-sponsored with surplus cash found from local good causes.)

Matt had gone to the rest room. As he added a dab of Moulton Brown to his towel-dried hands, a sudden "Aaaah!" followed by a crash and a cubicle door springing open, gave him a shock.

Two half-naked bodies, perfectly hooked and hinged at the centre, collapsed to the marble-paved ground – barely missing their heads. One torso belonged to an agency Associate Creative Director of Communications (AC/DC). The wife of the *Jeet Kun Do* master claimed the second body.

Matt wasn't sure if he should offer to pull one out of the other (he prided himself in problem solving). He decided that it was best to leave things be. He spent the following six minutes standing outside the rest rooms telling would-be visitors that the facilities were out of order. At the close of his guard duty, Matt stepped aside as the couple left separately to return to the table. By then the conversation had reached the "fully restored out-house" stage.

Matt kept the AC/DC on. The client was happy that his wife began showing a little interest in his affairs. She even chipped in some expensive, but fascinating advertising ideas.

In addition to chances for Suits to open client gifts of Moët and creative directors to wipe their hands in prestigious rest rooms, there were the annual departmental dinners and a seasonal discos open to the lower echelons. Department team members covered the cost of set-menu food. The agency footed up to a £150 bar tab per team.

Every January (managers were already totally booked during December) a 'Big Night Bash' featured a disco by 'Barry's Lounge'. By day, Barry (whose real name was Sydney) was a serious and scrupulous accountant. He heralded from the original legendary Jamie Dow mashup days (mostly nights). Come street-lighting time, Barry scuttled out of his orderly City office, lined with accountancy rulebooks, to emerge as an ageless musical zealot. His choices, from Led Zeppelin and Pink Floyd to Skream and Torbjørn Brundtland, were so eclectic that everyone couldn't help but get into the groove and escape the grind.

Sam admired Barry's ability to sift through Schedule 7AC of the 'Taxation of Chargeable Gains Act 1992' and still be awake to spin music at night. As with Jamie, Sam's old friend who turned from boardroom research tsar to police-busted warehouse rave DJ, Barry gave him hope.

Additionally, each year the latest Edinburgh Comedy Festival winner (recommended by Daniel Rix, a brilliant spotter and manager of gifted speakers) delivered bowdlerised cracks about management, the IT help desk, as well as the competition.

To further ensure that underpaid teams and fidgety freelancers complied with agency worker regulations, Alice hired her own crack team of 'HR' (holiday-rota) enforcers. Not only did these fighters against freedom ruthlessly terminate requests to take the family to Crete during the first week of August, but acting with dispassionate sincerity, also:

- Cooed at, and with, newbies.
- Explained where the milk was kept to the newbies (alongside the unbreakable rule to clean and replace their cups in the cupboard).
- Noted people who laughed too much when they gathered as a group in the corridor (a possible indication of harassment towards new staff).
- Offered reassuring smiles to established staff.
- Walked undeterred through a department, without flinching at any contemptuous looks.
- Policed recruitment processes in accordance with the 'Banana Rule'.

The banana rule dictated that, irrespective of a candidate's experience, talent or potential, HR should consider only those precisely matching an official written 'crew opportunity' description.

For example, should a creative manager request a photographer for a banana shoot, even if an applicant had awards, should their showcase portfolio not include a picture of a banana, or feature photos that may contravene client or agency creative expectations of said banana, the applicant should be tactfully precluded and offered to have their application 'put on file'.

Other small print that took back what the big print gave included:

(D)

Be fully compliant with key principles of current company law regarding unfair dismissal. (Available on the HR intranet. Such principles include: employee political or religious activism, harassment, contract intricacies, workplace accidents, use and responsibility of company property, intellectual property rights, company representation liability, professional conduct, expense dues, slander, liability and injury claims.)

(E)

Discourage 'Cubicle Vultures' by forensic cleansing of evidence suggesting a messy firing: vacated workstations must be spotless; ex-employee's password revoked; e-mail re-routed and reviewed for the last three months. Provocative correspondence, including social network entries on Twitter and Facebook (including Facebook Timeline archives), should be backed up for future possible litigation reference (as detailed in task 'D').

The ever-taunting *schadenfreude* directed at those with less, from those with slightly more, added to the general sense of gratitude for having a job – any job.

The rich cherished quality at prices that no one else could afford. The rest valued quantity at prices that couldn't be beaten.

Everyone pulled together to bring in the profits for the good of the greater whole, and financial riches for the chosen few.

Chapter 14

For a price (of sorts), Sam willingly shared with other CEOs his flair for public and employee approbation. He arranged for the wittiest, most self-deprecating, yet brilliantly insightful blogs to be written on behalf of fellow chairmen needing to satisfy potential clients, journalists or existing shareholders. CEOs, many with companies quoted from the FTSE to the NYSE, the DAX to the Hang Seng, were indexed in Sam's personal file of favours to be returned – with interest (fiscal or otherwise).

His network included 'independent' agencies that were conveniently distant from the group to provide unbiased recommendations and services for clients.

Amongst the 'independents' was CPC (Croughterman Public Consciousness). The agency was led by Colin Croughterman. He wore a short, mauve ponytail that dangled beneath a mane of once curly golden hair. His 'right on' attitude and narrow designer glasses went down well with the crowd. Add an eclectic circus of operatic, sporting, burlesque, fashion, broadcasting and celebrity connections, even the occasional presidential candidate entangled in sexual, financial or criminal allegations, and people were hooked to the ringmaster's magnetism. In return, Colin ensured that prying press and paying clients were kept poles apart.

Watching Colin's earthy, anarchic lectures to PR graduates on YouTube convinced Sam to merge CPC into his circle of 'Detail Developers'.

When required, Colin ranted and tweeted about "the propaganda of the improbable to the impressionable". His blogged hoop-la and press Twitterviews were encoded with ingeniously indexed algorithms. Tirades were easy to find, virals simple to spread, and the mavens who scanned them even easier to track.

Colin's preaching made him a man of the cloth, albeit a leather cloth. As one of the best Spokesweasels in the business, he knew how to whip up a cause, where to crack the whip and who provided the finest Kangaroo leather to unleash the loudest shot.

Crusades mostly featured either hitherto undisclosed facts about the recklessly powerful, scams by business people who politicians described as "just good friends" or public meltdowns of a former luminary searching for an audience to re-ignite their fading nine-volt battery lamp.

Colin's biggest accounts were media clients. CPC's extravaganza of entrepreneurs, newspapers, gossips sites, and production companies relied on sturdy audience figures.

To placate advertisers, Colin gave moguls soundbite press conferences or official inquiry apologies. The apologies were hacked by hacks. "I apologise profusely. 'Principles before profits' will be our new mantra," a penitent media proprietor would read (mixing his 'principles' with his 'principals').

A common fix for a supernova celebrity or overcooked sun flare was to toss either into a vipers' pit: *Strictly Come Dancing* or *I'm a Celebrity Get Me Out of Here* were typical planetariums or fish bowls (depending on the scale, weight and allure of the celeb).

Full frontal strip downs were gangoozled throughout the nation of 'press the red-button for details' fidgets. The celebrity's torment, albeit titillating, confirmed that, just as the fidgets suspected, once defrocked of status, the celeb was little more than a casserole of flesh, bones and pangs (like many of the viewers themselves).

The public humiliation masochistically satisfied the celebrity's bare ambition to win at any cost. Before long, CPC had a book published called *All About Me* (ghost-written by a wealthy self-help and brand back story writer).

Next up: a self-esteem support website. Later, revelations about football players or ball foot playing public figures were added to the stew. If by then CPC's clients were still on a winner with the loser, a movie deal, or at least a YouTube series, could be in the sewage pipework.

Further campaigns were manufactured, packaged and delivered with pin-sharp logistics to any anonymous patrons or corporate ballers carrying enough readies to glorify corporate reputations and initiatives. The majority of business crusades wanted to expose competitors whose ideas breached bottom-line perceptions, and therefore profits.

Apart from an up-front fee, clients required sufficient motivation spurred on by any combination of greed, avarice, single-mindedness, ambition, boredom, frustration, social exclusion, loneliness, vanity, self-loathing, anger, concern, disappointment, conceit, responsibility, uncertainty, status, revenge or inadequacy. Beyond all else, punters needed obdurate faith to commit to a 120-year mortgage on 15 minutes of fame (guaranteed) as relished by them or regretted by competitors.

CPC's arsenal included smuggled footage, handsome girls, pretty boys, clandestine recordings or, thanks to Colin's photojournalism contacts, Canon EF 600mm f/4L IS II USM super-telephoto lens snapshots of closely guarded secrets hitherto kept in the government's Cabinet or CEO's executive bathroom.

Colin's greatest weapon was his 'little black book' of indiscrete confessions. If needed, investigative reporters would be given a tip-off based on secrets that slithered out from within the book's snakeskin cover.

The hack's meticulous reportage poured the exact measure of social consciousness required to win votes, boost confidence, endear loyalty, encourage unity, steal sales or deliver high audience ratings: brands were happy. CPC's patrons remained quietly confident of another sponsorship season.

Sam's detail developers were widespread. Through them sealed public investigation committee room doors were open. Innovators, believers, coders, developers, achievers, breakers, makers... were given the spotlight they craved since their adolescent days, when with torch in one hand, they lurched back and forth under a bed sheet. With humility, each now stood in front of TED audiences willing to pay fortunes for front row seats of explosive erudition.

New truths were noted on diminutive notepads or dimmable tablets. Everyone was galvanised by homilies that urged them never to give up scaling fences, however distant or far.

Anything was possible at the place where legends began and names were built: the market stall of Messrs Barnes and Roberts.

בראשית

IN THE BEGINNING

Chapter 1

Sam settled into his multi-adjustable Girsberger Trilax 2 throne. Dancing his fingers on the Apple track pad, he tapped and tracked the latest trickles of Arab brooks. Editorial comment supported 'live tubed' coverage from on-the-scene reporters who had trained and waited an entire career to wear an oversized black helmet and flack jacket.

According to intelligence briefings, the latest despot, from a long line of King Canutes, was currently an ally. Future briefings may recommend Foreign Office spokespeople to describe him from a choice of alternative adjectives including: *irascible, manic, deranged, warm, reformed, captivating, tireless, obdurate, curious, statesmanlike, fearless, exotic, bizarre, evil, idiosyncratic, ruthless* and, of course, *brutal* (a perennial favourite with the hack-flack-jacks). The current despot's methods were a little dodgy but (according to the news editorial) understandable – "given the region's history".

In return for patronage from a coalition of political and commercial empire builders, the King/General/President/Commander ensured that whichever dusty or overgrown battlefield the Coalition decided to park their latest high tech tanks on, the vehicles would still be there, in one piece, when drivers returned from a comfort break.

"Same old…" Sam concluded.

Of far more interest was a UK airline's advert. It sat besides an article describing the recent triumphant win of the English cricket team. The ad had been part of a build-up campaign to the 2012 Olympics. The first stage addressed the airline's heritage. *Decades of service: flights of pride* read the headlines.

The ads featured a mashup of British landmarks and symbols, together with pictures of cabin crew, past and present. One ad showed a Cornish pasty on a red, white and blue dish. Originally the creative director (a vegetarian) suggested an Eccles cake. In the end the pasty was chosen: not only was it more popular than even a black pudding, but narrowly beat a Kendal cake to the top spot. A 'consultant' TV chef especially sequestered for the project put the final winner's success down to the pasty's roughly cut chunks of British beef.

The next stage of the campaign promoted the carrier's dual sponsorship of the Olympics and Paralympics, along with being the British Monarchy's preferred airline: 2012 also marked Her Majesty the Queen's Diamond Jubilee, at which the airline flew a 1952 de Havilland Comet over the official River Thames pageant.

The campaign featured flaming torches, courageous athletes and airplanes leaving red, white and blue vapour streams above the multi-billion Olympic legacies.

The follow-up campaign to the Games set a flight path towards the future: "We gave wings to winners. We give hope to reel in gold."

'Winged Winners' (described in the search engine-optimised ad as 'home grown visionaries in the arts') were awarded grants and publicity. Exposure included having their paintings displayed in the airline's business class lounges (rebranded 'Club Avancé').

More PR was pressed from initiatives, including a special 'Winged Winners' edition in-flight magazine. In addition to a receiving a cheque for £10,000 for an inspirational story of endurance, the 'winged' author was presented with a framed copy of the magazine. It was nestled inside a brand-design approved, midnight-blue coloured mount featuring a brass 'blank' emblazoned with the airline's name and logo.

The £10k paid off the author's Barclaycard bills, loans from friends and rent. He even bagged a weekend deal on lastminute.com. It included a return easyJet flight and B&B at a three star hotel up the road from the Maison de Balzac Museum.

The framed magazine finally ended up in the same spare room where the author had spent the previous two years with his head in the clouds, ear canal docked into Ed Sheeran, and fingers on a yellowing Toshiba keyboard.

… A further tap on Sam's trackpad: another advert from an Olympic sponsor; the global Trade and Overseas Energy corporation. The giant TOE (a client of one of the group's specialist industrial agencies) had invested £7.8m towards an environmentally sustainable 'breathable cavity scarf'. The carbon structure featured resins prepared by its Polyacrylate Performance Section. Previously, sodium polyacrylate had been used in producing tampon and diapers. However, whilst superbly efficient in absorbing oils and moisture, the 'scarf' often left painful rashes on an installer's hands.

Malcolm Brent, the head of B&R's industrial agency, 'Cogs', ensured that TOE's achievement was advertised throughout the trade's bio life sciences network. When Malcolm introduced Sam to the client, the globally recognised corporation was suffering from a fungal infection of public cynicism. Dubious alleged business associations tenuously linked the brand to a completely different organisation. (An alleged act of sabotage at the other company's plant claimed over 10,000 lives).

In 2011, announcing the eco-friendly Olympics sponsorship, a CPC media-trained TOE spokesperson announced: "Today, the honour of being a worldwide Olympic partner reflects our realisation of a bio-tech future."

Sam paused for a few seconds to admire Cogs' design team's typeface choice: Johan Aakerlund's Comfortaa 18pt high font. It spelt out the slogan:

Peace, progress, and sustainability – celebrating the human race.

… Martha's '10.30' intercom announcement interrupted his train of thought.

The door was flung open.

"Woot 12!" exclaimed Matt, making a straight line for the gumball machine. "We're cooking…"

"… With gas," Sam said, completing the slogan from years back.

Ah, Matt's hooey, Sam thought to himself, as his business partner popped another red, yellow and green.

Matt was in his late forties. To those who didn't know him, he had the zeal (if not the looks) of a 30 year old, going on 37.

As with the commas shuffling along Charlotte Street, Matt's hairline was receding. He wore his customary blue jeans. Today's shirt choice was a cappuccino cream, with subtle brown pinstripes, framed by a Brooks Brothers' Madison Fit Cashmere Check blazer.

Leaning against the 'Mouthy Marvin', Matt got down to business. He handed Sam a file: '12'.

It was the final treatment prescribed for a deep-rooted and potentially terminal malady first analysed on a chilly February morning in 2010. The condition's aetiology went back way further.

Chapter 2

Double-dip recessions and boomerangs shared many similarities: firstly, their shape; secondly, both had the disconcerting habit, that no matter how far away they were lobbed, both returned when least expected to give their knowledgeable tossers a bang on the head.

As with Sam, Matt understood the psychology of markets and men. If a man's mind became fixated on avoiding driving towards danger, his hands steered him towards it. When markets lost confidence, uncertainty gained conviction. For years, global advertising revenues had steadily plunged. Despite good initial online sales, fads turned into trends that transformed into feet stuck fast in sticky puddings.

Many agencies haemorrhaged clients to more affordable garage-based web designers, maverick social media planners and former big brand executives. In response, the agencies invested in buying out any breakaway talent that threatened to become competitors. To stay in the game, everything at any price was up for grabs.

With huge overheads, the biggest agencies were left competing with as many leaner players as their bank loans could attack. Whereas once they enjoyed reputations as quick and smart thinkers, the bureaucracy involved with running massive operations meant they no longer had time to imagine possibilities. They became USS *Gerald R. Ford* aircraft carriers: fully prepared to despatch fire-fighting missions around the world, whilst needing as much time and space as possible to come to a pause and think.

That kind of conjecture was too slow for the new, impulsive market. Compulsive consumerism led people to treat product upgrades as bosses treated them, and shareholders treated the bosses: 'disposables', once underpowered, or worn-out commodities, were trashed or trafficked via eBay or executive recruitment sites.

Constant drip after drip infusions from online ads overwhelmed the superhighway with companies prepared to do whatever it took to win the attention of an easily bored or credit-snapped public.

Eventually, even big-name brands concentrated on selling to idiosyncratic markets:

Jimmy Choos – People with ample credit to flaunt their feats of success.

Clarks – The 'squeezed middle', acclimatising to replacement leather insoles, rather than brand new shoes.

Shoe Zone – Taking pride in keeping their money safely wrapped inside wallets, rather than around their feet.

Some envied others. Others wanted to slip on someone else's ID (if only for one night). Realising the value of Oscar Wilde's advice to be themselves (as everyone else was already taken), plenty stood up to claim that the right to walk in their own boots was worth its weight in leather. Over time, everyone's cupboards had at least four boxes of empty shoes.

A fourth group, that couldn't even afford shoes, whinged about everyone else – until they met a fifth group that had no feet at all.

Chapter 3

Outside, it was one of the coldest February mornings on record. Inside, Sam and Matt carried their Starbucks' 'Talls' towards a table occupied by Barnes and Roberts' fidgety 32-year-old Head of Research and Planning, Ben Josephs.

Amongst other formal skills, he was a promising cartoonist. Back in the day, his vicious style went down a treat in the student rag. Seeing the approaching duo, Ben flipped over a doodle. Once settled into the conversation, he pointed Sam and Matt to a paper from the University of California, San Diego.

"In terms of data consumption alone, America is already getting through 3.6 zettabytes a day," explained Ben.

"Fascinating," Matt muttered, stirring his drink with a Starbucks lolly stick.

"Think of it like this: America is gobbling up the equivalent of at least sixteen hard drives for every man, woman and child in the US…" Ben continued.

Matt lapped the froth from the stick.

"That's like an entire series of *Curb Your Enthusiasm* but crammed into one day," Ben patiently explained.

Matt stopped slurping.

Ben pulled out a printed infographic previously sketched on his

Wacom. It traced back to when advertisers 'pushed' brand messages at people. Once that stopped working, consumers 'pulled' what they wanted, when they wanted it.

"So many ads looking to be pulled on a first date left consumers dazed," Ben explained, pointing to the contorted cartoons of a consumer.

"People didn't want to risk getting into long-term relationships let alone a dinner date," Ben added, recalling a fit contestant on last night's *Come Dine With Me.*

"Even now, B2Bs are swamped with offers of free white papers or Webinars. Consumer email campaigns are not much better. Every subject box offers contains 'Last chance, final offer, hurry before it's too late…'"

"Viagra and Cialis," added Matt.

Sam smiled.

"Yeah, those too," laughed Ben. "Either way, they all trigger off spam hunters that dispatch them direct to Trashcan heaven."

Ben came close to nailing it. Wherever consumers connected on sites like Pinterest, or shared their creativity with Apps like Instagram, brands soon followed. As the years passed, highly paid 'white hats' weaned on jail breaking PlayStations, ensured brands sent out an intensified onslaught of offers. A casual visit to a site or social space dispatched an arachnosquad of spiders evolved to offer a tantalizing lure based on specifically calculated patterns of surfing behaviour. A return visit guaranteed a plague of web crawlers.

Meanwhile 'black hat' highway hackers attacked ever-sprawling communication lines carrying everything from credit card details, to national defence codes. With so many tracks connecting so many stations, every moment was high noon in the battle of the 'white hats', 'grey hats' and 'black hats'.

Sam chipped in: "But 'pull' gave – gives – choice. That's never a bad thing... at least from their point view. Besides, even as Facebook's usage finally levels out, we've got more tools up our sleeves. Gamification for one thing; or as I like to call it, 'consumer grooming'."

"Consumer grooming?" Matt inquired, getting drawn further into the conversation.

"It's when you put out a free game or something similar to attract the consumer. You invite them to complete something, they get involved. Game on... Next up comes engagement. They give away more personal details. Finally, clicking the 'buy' button, they bite. Game over."

"That's just perverted!" Matt scoffed.

"I'm with Matt," Ben agreed. "Anyways, more people mean more ignored ads. Eventually even gamification will have to throw down its cards. Folks get peeved when brand zombies crawl into their social space."

"It's alive, it's moving... it's alive! An uncontainable Frankenstein," Matt precipitously groaned.

"Ah ha..." Sam replied, recalling the line from the Boris Karloff classic. "The brain is useless. We must find another brain!"

Raising his cup, Matt saluted Sam's contribution and long-term memory – which, he spotted, was on top form.

Ben shook his head with mock exasperation.

"The fact is, without direction you get a mobocracy," he continued. "The sheep start herding the shepherd. Lack of confidence, leaders screwing up, oil companies spilling magic beans off former idyllic coastlines... by this time next year we'll be back on the downhill drop."

"Surely you still trust me?" Sam cackled.

"There's always an exception to every rule," Ben replied diplomatically, before instinctively returning to doodling.

Beyond the bravado, like generations of business people before him, Sam recognised the plot line. Twelve days prior to the Great Depression of 1929, America's foremost economist, Yale Professor Irving Fisher, had proclaimed: "Stocks have reached what looks like a permanently high plateau." Those same stocks didn't stop tumbling from one precipice to the next until 1933, when president Franklin Delano Roosevelt temporarily closed all the banks.

During his own lifetime, Sam saw slumps droop and rise; advertising budgets stand and fall.

"It's not as if business, politics or the media have operated any differently from in the past," Sam reasoned.

Matt agreed. Bankers still advertised penny saving products to plebs, whilst keeping the most profitable investments for the bank's top brass.

As ever, politicians campaigned for greater austerity, stronger citizenship and firmer control away from institutions. If voters became too cynical, politicians could always turn mob disillusionment into collective delight by picking a war with another nation – especially if it could be 'sold' as protecting the nation's honour.

Sam had the familiar angles covered. Thanks to the lobbying shamanism of people like Colin – judiciously topped up with insidious party funding – institutions retained enough discreet control over the politicians to sway policies without raising suspicions.

Chapter 4

SAM KNEW THAT LIFE and business were cyclical. Each January, viewers switched on recently purchased plasma TVs to watch breakfast show presenters promote the latest celebrity comeback fitness DVD (displayed on the show's coffee table).

Slapping on the grease paint to give it one more shot, the celebrity ball-bouncing, Zumba swinging, hyper-charged, fitness boot camp trainer urged viewers to thrust their hips with greater gusto. Formerly a dancing show contestant, prior to that, a talk show host, previous soap actor, prior singer, former astrologist, and earlier Butlin's talent show winner, the celeb had a misunderstood youth. She just wanted to wear the right labels, as seen on TV.

The breathless star-jumper would have already invested any advanced DVD royalties into five months' of personal training. Long and sweaty jogging sessions, complemented by binging, puking and regular twists on an 'Abs 'n' Buns' exerciser, would have turned a depressed doughnut craver into a dynamic slimmer of the year. (So far, all five days of it.)

Six weeks following the DVD's initial release, overstocked discs would be bulk-sold to charity shops.

The discontinued DVDs signalled the beginning of the Valentine's Day season. This time, the breakfast presenters' coffee table featured a vase of roses. The presenters winced jovially at the weather girls' quip: "What's a ram's favourite Valentine's song? – I only have eyes for ewe, dear…" Wondering who actually wrote this material, the presenters battled on with the auto-queue that scrolled details of a romantic Brussels-based, prize weekend (courtesy of EuroStar and Interflora).

Viewers had to complete the phrase: what comes after 'Valentine's_____.

A) Day

B) Night

C) … spent three hours driving around looking for a restaurant that didn't require a previous booking

D) TV dinner for one

In return for their wisdom and £1.91 telephone charges per minute (each call lasting no more than five minutes), a lucky winning couple could anticipate strolling arm-in-arm around La Grand-Place, feeding each other truffles from a Hotel du Nougatine special selection box.

And still the buying clock ticked…

… Within weeks, the talk between the hosts sat on the burnt orange-coloured TV breakfast sofa would be of homemade back-to-basics recipes. The instructions were devised by a cockney-sounding Italian. His imperial range of pots and pans were licensed to multi-national emporiums via an artful brand label powerhouse.

As sure as over-stewed broccoli turns to gunk, by summer (high season for remaindered celebrity cookbooks) the 'buy junk' channels would join the mass-selling trail.

The lovely Alison (a size 18 shopping-channel 'friend') demonstrated a remarkable tummy-flattening bikini girdle, reinforced with woven Kevlar. It was just 16 credit card numbers plus £5 p&p away for like-waisted, 'large boned' housewives.

With bargain priced bikinis packed in vacuum-sealed shrink-wraps, the golden sun outside the nation's tightly-drawn curtains (to get a better picture on the telly) blended into a copper-penny autumn.

… And still marketing algorithms measuring periods, location, history and habits, relentlessly led the way for brands whose heads of staff used data to justify increased marketing budgets, or better still, salary bonuses.

This time, ads offered short-break holiday consolations to home shoppers who couldn't afford a summer holiday or credit control clerks who would never finally complete the 'pending pile'. The getaways promised a lift to the teary-eyed administrators whose screensavers showed iPhoto memories of holidays in Faliraki.

During Diwali, night skies ignited with neon-bathed bargains that glittered well into extended festival shopping hours.

Then came the Season of Goodwill's turn.

Commercials featured crackling firesides and choirs of cherubs led by either the cockney chef, a saggy Santa or a 'neutrally appropriate' animated character. Singing in the style of a heavenly Christmas song by Eric Idle, the choristers praised merchandising's monarchy for bearing gifts online.

Finally, completing the year's usual 365.25 day cycle, 1st January reappeared.

At 7 a.m. a 3D-HDTV with online access, purchased at the pre-Xmas, pre-New Year sales, would flicker to life in front of a devastated room, scattered with broken toys, an upturned 'next gen' console and red wine carpet stains.

Sandwiched between the HDTV's glass and microchips, breakfast show interviewers chatted about a former soap star's 'breakthrough' diet download as well as the exciting new series of *Gluttons: Stop or Die.*

At that time of the morning, apart from pensioners chewing grapes, the only audience would be either toddlers smashing repeatedly the head of a doll on the floor, or unconscious teenagers, overdosed on all night remixes of Camo & Krooked.

As the toddler made his way to the console, a cheerful money-saving website 'guru' joined the breakfast duo with advice on shrewd credit card management tactics.

… And so started a whole new year of broken resolutions.

Matt, too, understood the game. He and Sam were in the business to make the probable profitable. The precise tension between predictability and possibility formed the backbone of everything.

… In Starbucks, Sam's, Matt's and Ben's 'Talls' had reached the thin wedge of the bottom of their cups. Time to wrap up. Ben drew the final touches to his sketch: a crude caricature of the British PM on the shoulders of the opposition leader, who clung to the US president, riding on the back of a giant mosquito, which fed on an outstretched tattooed arm, whose Textur font spelt: 𝕬𝖘𝖎𝖆: 𝕿𝖍𝖊 𝕱𝖎𝖓𝖆𝖑 𝕱𝖗𝖔𝖓𝖙𝖎𝖊𝖗.

Chapter 5

Months after the Starbucks meeting, Sam and Matt dropped by their own coffee hangout: the Think Tank.

"You know," whispered Sam (mindful of the waddling 'Ricos', to whom he nodded a smile), "in the old days, original campaigns enjoyed prosperous shelf lives. They stood up. Ben was right. Today, clients are so risk adverse, there's nothing fresh. Campaigns get copied or parodied to the point that frankly, it's all just more orbiting space junk that eventually crashes on some poor bastard's Honda in the driveway."

"Well, at least we've got a crash helmet," said Matt, offering his own brand of practical philosophy.

"It's like sex and Christmas," Sam added dunking a madeleine cake into his cup.

Matt was intrigued.

"… It's about anticipation for the moment," explained Sam.

"Unless you're talking about pulling a cracker, I don't think the two immediately go together," Matt said.

Sam tittered at Matt's cheesy joke, then continued: "Come or go, everybody wants it. At some point, they wonder how everyone else does it. But most of all, what's going to be revealed beneath the shirt or blouse. Which, apart from some German web exceptions, turns out to be predictably the same."

"And Christmas?" Matt asked.

"When it comes to love, giving is a greater pleasure than receiving."

They both chuckled.

From the corner of his eye Sam became distracted by a man sat at a table. The man always seemed to be in the Think Tank whenever Sam dropped by.

(Sensing his nibs' surveillance, Gary shifted uncomfortably in his seat.)

"We need a new recipe – something for everyone," Sam said.

"Recipe?"

A shudder ran through Sam's whole body.

"… With a wonderful ingredient shaded smoky-pink and silver."

Sam opened his iPad and unlocked the personal contact details of CEOs and corporate presidents from various agencies. Grinning, he watched Gary busily flick through a wad of papers piled next to his own iPad. Sam suspected the tablet had been used to check out Germany's latest falls and rises.

Chapter 6

Today's '3.30': NANCY SANDERSON was eight minutes early. Martha took Nancy's Evans purchased coat. At precisely 3.30, Martha buzzed Sam that Ms Sanderson had arrived.

Sam led the journalist to the Carol Bimbi. Nancy immediately spotted the creamy-white topping that revealed just a hint of the red, moist treasure beneath. To ease her torment, she focused every ounce of effort onto a chipped nail that bit into her Essie Plumberry painted left thumb… anything to avert her eyes from the gorgeous vanilla fondant sprawled across one of the K&Cs begging to be lapped and loved.

"Can I interest you in a cupcake, Nancy?" Sam asked.

"Thanks – but I really shouldn't."

"Seems a waste. I fancy one. Love them actually."

"You are a very bad person Samuel Roberts," Nancy replied, reaching for a 'Red Velvet'. (She promised herself to skip tomorrow's double-chocolate Kit-Kat.)

Nancy was part of CNN's crew. She knew the business, stretching back to when Colonel Muammar Gaddafi had his head in the clouds, rather than body in the sand; even before G.H.W. first crossed swords with Saddam or uranium was a glint in Mahmoud Ahmadinejad's eyes.

Her war with weight had raged for as long as she could remember. Most girls at Uni concentrated on either pitching to, or ditching, the next would-be college baseball boyfriend. Nancy, on the other hand, was drawn to the world of comparative politics. (Not exactly a 'can of corn' for the boys looking to nail the game.)

She graduated from the University of Virginia in Charlottesville. Lectures covered a global parliament of political styles, reaching across Europe to Latin America, the Middle East, South Africa and various Eastern stops along the way.

Three dates temporarily diverted her from concentrating exclusively on Eda Saburo and the Japan Socialist Party. Each occasion lasted approximately four weeks. The first, with a guy called Greg, mostly involved long talks on route to the 29 Diner. Once there, they drank malt shakes and she listened to his theories on Jack Kerouac. The relationship ended when Greg turned up drunk.

The second date was sweet but ultimately sobering. His degree was drawing towards an end. One day in late June, Nancy received a note saying he was catching a Greyhound to Jackson, Mississippi, where two kids had been caught up in a riot. (Nancy figured the journey must have taken at least 14 hours.)

He didn't return. Years passed before they inadvertently caught up. They instantly recognised each other at a Mississippi press meeting held at the Gold Parlour room in the governor's mansion. Pleasantries were exchanged but little else.

Finally there was Chuck. If it weren't for Nancy feeling peckish, Chuck would never have met his wife.

The story started at a Bob Dylan concert in the John Paul Jones arena. During the half-show break, Chuck offered to get Nancy a hotdog. Whilst she remained in the main arena watching the crowds, Chuck was in the corridors talking to the cart owner's wife (who was emptying a nearby trashcan that filled as quickly as her husband could cook up bun pups).

Chuck returned with the hotdog. Nancy wanted extra onions. Chuck quickly offered to return with extra relish.

That was that. Two months later, Chuck dropped his promising academic career in foreign affairs for the cook's wife.

Whilst former cheerleaders from Nancy's Uni went on to juggle dazzling PR careers during the day with dirty nappies at night, Nancy became a self-assured, senior producer.

Her ability to smell a bad onion, or spot an overcooked wiener from a gas bag, won her the nickname of 'Oreo': she appeared hard on the outside, but at heart, was a softie. In terms of sheer professionalism Nancy always delivered.

Sam was no 'New York Push Cart'. Sure, he was smiles, charm and moves. But Nancy sensed there was more. They met decades back. She was putting together a piece for WSJ on Madonna's brand image. Sam's connections – including an exclusive interview and three sealed pre-publication copies of 'Sex', ensured a permanent place in her tab of useful contacts. Eventually those books (she kept two) could fetch £1k. But Sam's influence was priceless.

She was in the West End office to discuss the latest rumblings on the Brand Fish story.

"So is it true that this logo fish concept has sprouted another scale?" asked Nancy, noticing the cupcake's unflawed strawberry nipple.

Sam played along. "Sorry, you're driving at what exactly?"

"Twelve," Nancy purred, licking a flake of fondant from her lips. "Sam – you can't keep down the story of how one of the world's biggest brands is teaming up with what to all intents and purposes are competitors. So how did you convince them, and why did they buy it?"

Sam smiled an awkward frown. "Did anyone ever tell you how good you really are?"

"Yeah, right," replied Nancy, spotting that charm again, along with recognising a setup when she saw one.

Nancy reached for her Korg. (Recommended by a friend who worked at the *News of the World* prior to *The Sun on Sunday*). Placing it on the table, she asked if it was OK to record the conversation (it was standard procedure).

Reluctantly, Sam agreed.

"The Brand Fish – or as you call it, 'Logo Fish' – isn't about any single brand. It's responsible companies giving back," Sam said.

"Together we serve you," Nancy replied, quoting the popular Brand Fish slogan.

"With the economy in such a mess, brands have wised up that unless they give, there's nothing to take."

"Yes, I've read all the press releases and attended the launches – but Sam, two per cent of all annual sales is one big payday," noted Nancy.

"Look at it like this: brands have big sway. If those brands can set examples, maybe even the politicians will follow suit."

"… And maybe one day Medicare will pay for Dolly Parton's boobs. Seriously, how do you intend to measure it all?" asked Nancy, thinking that Sam would have made quite a politician himself.

"As the press has said – and Nancy my love, I know that you already know – in addition to OWA-9, the entire project is carefully audited to the last decimal. Each individual brand's sales are calculated from the moment they sign up to the project and whether they have agreed to be part of the campaign on a global, regional or country-by-country basis," Sam explained.

"… Encouraging more spend on advertising and PR," Nancy said, considering going for a second cup.

"If you're a cynic I suppose…"

"Surely, any measure will be affected by more than just the 'Logo' – sorry, 'Brand Fish' – campaign. Besides, is this twelfth addition in on a global, or country-by-country footing?"

"EMEA," Sam answered, wondering if she would rise to another K&C.

Sensing that she was about to bite the Brand Fish bait, Sam continued.

"The point here is that we have put together the world's greatest brand names who, for once, are combining to make a difference. Besides, it's all incredibly democratic. Charities are nominated by each brand's customer base."

"The 'Fishing for Gold' campaign after the last Olympics…" Nancy remembered, refusing to be drawn by the remaining K&Cs.

"Precisely."

Sam's phone rang.

He ignored it.

Estimated donations and signed-up causes noted, Nancy thanked Sam for his time. She decided that if she played nice, he would give her the green light for a bigger exclusive later.

After a parting glance at the K&Cs, she packed the Korg away.

"You know," she added, hand hovering on the door handle, "I still think the whole fish thing is one very smart piece of PR. The big question will be if the public buy or let it swim away with the tide."

Sam gave Nancy a peck on the cheek. "Forever the sceptic."

"For always the journalist," Nancy replied.

"As every salmon knows, only dead fish swim with the stream. Right now, we all have to swim that bit harder."

"Yeah, I can see things are tough for you," Nancy said, glancing at the nimbly trimmed bonsai trees on the SMA bookshelf. Then, making a mental note of the salmon quote, she left.

Sam wasn't lying. The project was about growth and concern. But he hadn't quite revealed the bigger picture. For example, he overlooked to mention that in the name of economising, global clients were offering less for more: cans of pop were drained from just under 500ml to 370ml.

Advertised lower costs suggested greater customer value. Without even realising it, the consumer was actually paying more for the volume of drink. Better still, smaller portions acted like samples that encouraged consumers to 'trade up' to bigger sizes (which, in actual fact, were smaller than their former advertised larger size).

As always, the facts were in the details. Occasion. Brand. Price. Pack. Channel: OBPPC. Offer the right portion at the right perceived price for the right occasion from a trusted brand and you were onto a winner. Besides, reduced portions with healthy price tags were even welcomed by the calorie watchers who responded by buying bigger packs of 'little treats'.

Dum Spiro, Spero, thought Sam as he massaged his upper neck. At some point in the day it always started to burn. To take his mind off it, he inspected the bonsai on the Primo.

Unlike technology, Bonsais didn't require App updates: just a little application of tender loving care.

Officially, the trees were not named 'bonsai'. They were mostly juniper trees. 'Bonsai' referred to the craft of regular pruning to keep them in shape. He opened a small wooden case that sat unobtrusively next to one of the trees. A velvet-lined trio of compartments held a butterfly shear, concave cutter and wire cutter. Regularly maintained with Japanese choji oil, each instrument was in impeccable condition.

Selecting the butterfly shear, Sam carefully pruned a pin-sized branch, then gingerly replaced the shear and stepped back to admire his grooming. One leaf was not perpendicularly perfect, but for now, he'd done a good job; still far more rewarding than indexing Apps into their boxes.

Back at his desk, Sam dropped the twig into a Nox Magnum wastebasket. He swivelled the Fiorenzo Dorigo towards the window. Down below, the commas were still on the move. Cleavages continued to alternate between revealing slanted lips and trembling smirks. Joining them was Nancy. She carried a ribbon-tied box containing three K&Cs prepared by 'M', presented with Sam's compliments.

A flick of his finger disclosed the share prices of each of the '12' Brand Fish project partners: yellows and greens; a good start. He checked the prices for the group's various media companies that offered the '12' special discounts. The average share price was 64.47. Not bad, considering last year's low of 49.53.

Nancy should really learn to follow her hunches, Sam thought. Still, the good Lord gives and takes.

"'M'," he asked, pressing the internal speaker. "That bottle of…"

"Chanel," completed 'M'. "Second shelf of the unit," she continued, "price removed, suitably bagged… and the rabbit – extra cuddly."

"Ah, the rabbit. Thanks." Sam said, looking forward to giving his baby a huge hug.

PART ◆ THREE

וישש

AND HE DREW NEAR

Chapter 1

Through the nets, Dan watched a harassed mother tugging at a young boy who flatly refused to go into Sainsbury's with her. Five minutes earlier, he had watched as she had withdrawn £70 from the Santander Bank cashpoint.

Bollocks, he thought. "Thank you, another day gone," he grumbled at the passing traffic below.

The modest flat was tidy. Amy liked it that way. Parquet flooring ran along every room – except the bathroom – which was actually a shower room, with a small wall cabinet from B&Q. In an attempt to match the rest of the flat's flooring scheme, it also included a toilet with a wooden seat.

A 3x5x4m kitchen featured a foldaway tabletop carrying Amy's Vaio. The 5x6.5m lounge included an Ikea Billy bookcase, two-seater sofa and Tofteryd bench holding a Sky+ box and Samsung flat screen. There were two bedrooms: one 4x3m, a second, 6x4m.

The Billy carried the usual assortment of books: *The Complete Works of Shakespeare*, Charles Dickens' *Great Expectations*, a few 1980s volumes of *Encyclopaedia Britannica*, *Roget's Thesaurus*, a ten-year-old copy of the *Concise Oxford Dictionary* and a King James' Bible. Space was left for delicately carved sculptures. One was a 27cm radius bowl of flowers, the other a 30cm high 'Eye of Ra' (exquisitely carved in sycamore).

As organisations increasingly "reconciled per capita productivity against market conditions" (slashed wages and resource costs), calls for Dan's talents had waned. Yet, he still had access to a Clerkenwell studio where friendships had been forged with fellow artisans. The Clerkenwell Workshop Cooperative was initially set up as a community of jewellers, metal workers, fabric designers, illustrators and bookbinders, including Cathy Nadeau.

She was married to an increasingly demoralised chiropodist. Cathy had made her name back in the late 1990s. Her handcrafted leather portfolio cases were used by the best photographers in town. As with Dan's work, calls for customised portfolios became increasingly sporadic. As craftspeople moved out, and online community processors moved in, so Cathy turned her skills to designing personalised leather or linen tablet computer covers. The work was welcomed, but profits were as flat as some of the feet that her husband scratched and sniffed each day.

Before the days of producers cutting down on film commissions, Dan was kept busy in his necessarily oversized workshop. He made a decent living carving replicas of everything from seventeenth-century bible boxes to sixteenth-century fireplace caryatids.

However, despite a 'money-expert' explaining on the radio that the average annual wages of FTSE CEOs had increased to £2.5 million, each passing month planed off a further slither of Dan's work. Luckily, he still received small commissions to ship private pieces to a CEO's holiday mansion. (Providing that, in keeping with the 'beat-down commerce' trend, the fee was kept rock bottom.)

Although prestigious, the private work was hardly profitable. A more enduring respite came courtesy of a BBC commission. The project was part of the Corporation's 'Cultural Olympiad' and the Queen's Diamond Jubilee. Special programmes included a season of Shakespeare's plays, a series exploring London's history and culture, as well as a four hour televised Jubilee concert culminating with the Queen firing a laser beam through a football-sized diamond of glass to light a beacon on Admiralty Arch. It wouldn't be the only laser display that year.

Dan was instructed to veneer in British oak an eight-metre circumference, plastic globe of the Earth. In addition to ostensibly being carved out of *solid* oak, the Earth had a hole bored between the spot marking the Olympic venue and its opposite side on the sphere. (In full scale, the hole would have emerged some 503.231 km from Campbell Island, near New Zealand.)

A projected beam of light was to rocket through the globe's centre and conveyed via various distribution points throughout the London skyline, finally reaching the official Olympic torch at the Game's East London venue.

Along with the Olympic torch being relayed through the capital, the BBC gave it a 'run-through' part in *Eastenders'* Albert Square. (The soap's fictitious square cleverly shared the same postcode as the real Olympic Park.)

The entire spectacular was in keeping with the Corporation's remit to "speak nation unto nation": plugging the world's ever widening abyss of empty national identities with British culture.

DAN MET AMY WHEN she was an assistant props master. Over a coffee served at the workshop's restaurant, she asked if he knew where to get a replica what-not built for a production of *The Case of the Silk Stocking*.

As Dan delivered his pitch, he noticed a cute tattoo on Amy's right arm.

"The Eye of Horus," she explained, picking up on his gaze. "Like it?"

"Nice. Does it mean something?" Dan pried.

"Kinda spiritual: the 'all-seeing eye'. It's supposed to bring whoever wears it safety, health, prosperity and wisdom."

"Neat."

"It makes me feel – I don't know – like someone is watching over me," Amy said, turning down her sleeve, shading the eye from the light.

Dan showed Amy around the studio. One look at the pieces convinced her of his talent. He landed the commission. His work put Amy in her boss's good books. Over two months, a local florist made a tidy profit sending out individual roses and the local Vue cinema doubled-up on Dan's movie and salted popcorn budget.

Six weeks in, sitting next to Dan, with tears slipping down her face, Amy squeezed his arm as, joining the rest of the audience at a re-run of *The Lion King* in 3D, they flew across Africa's plains. Two weeks later, in a modest room of a shared house near Waitrose in Chiswick, Dan's lounge side table received a wooden picture frame. His sheets were dressed with comfy new pillows from the appropriately named 'Daniel's Beds' store; the rest was history.

That was five years ago. Nowadays, the picture frame sat next to the Sky+ plus box in their Balham flat. The frame displayed a picture of the couple screaming on Alton Towers' Nemesis ride.

Although 'officially' on the dole, Dan occasionally picked up small cash-in-hand commissions. They were mostly from friends of friends who wanted something special for an anniversary or office. Thanks to Amy's support, and the workshop's landlord, who still hadn't found a new tenant for the studio, Dan could still use the studio to work on experimental designs which no one would ever have the vision to commission.

Most days, whenever he wasn't at the studio, his agenda followed a standard schedule:

Coffee
Nothing to Declare
Maury
Stagejobspro.com
Coffee
Hotmail to Amy (daily)
Bargain Hunt
Coffee
Heinz Soup
Facebook with Cathy (once a month)
bbcnews.co.uk
Countdown
Tweet catch up with @shinybicuit (whenever he fancied)
Coffee
Johnny Test
Model Town
London Tonight
Take away (call/stroll)
Amy

Opening the front door to Amy invariably bought a smile to Dan's face.

"Fish and flips?" she asked, sniffing sweet cod roe from the Parade Fish Bar wafting in from the lounge.

"Got it in one," Dan replied. "It's been ages since we last had it. For once, I fancied something different from yet another salad thing."

"I forgive you, babe," Amy said, running her hand through Dan's thick, wavy hair.

Sitting at the table, Amy stole a chip from Dan's bag. (She never ate chips – well, not 'officially'.)

"Anyhow," she continued, pilfering another chip, "we have something to celebrate."

Dan took a gulp of DC from the can.

"Celebrate?" he croaked, holding back a bubbly burp.

"Don't panic! There's no cross on a Clearblue!" Amy laughed, idly dipping a third chip into a small paper container of curry sauce.

"Listen. I am not panicking about responsibility…"

"Muzzle your nuzzle for a second," Amy said. "It's something else. Something came up at work with the Zeus account."

"A raise? You're not off the account?"

"Nope. Neither. But there's an opportunity, and it pays."

"Have you been head-hunted? With the hours they put you through, I'm not surprised," Dan added, noticing his hill of chips had collapsed into a heap.

"The Zeus global roadshow is still kicking, but getting bigger. The agency's even got Dean Dempsey from Multiply on the project. Amazing stuff. Live holograms at the O2. They're looking for a classy, really upmarket image."

"So…" Dan said.

"… So, the client has 'requested' a ten-metre-long carved

wooden logo. What the client wants, the client gets," Amy said nonchalantly.

"You kidding me? But why wood? The bloody thing would weigh a ton. Besides, they could make it out of plastic with a veneer – like I did for the Beeb. Even polystyrene… scene board… chipboard or, come to think of it, plywood would be cheaper."

"Class they want, chic they get. It came out of some data-driven knowledge perceptivity stuff. The brand needs to show 'authenticity and natural quality'. A statement demonstrating total social wholeness."

"'Data-driven knowledge perceptivity'… 'social wholeness'. You really do talk a lot of crap," Dan teased. "Besides, what's it got to do with a bloody huge lightning bolt logo carved out of solid wood?"

"Look, all you need to know, my love, is that you're making and selling it. Actually, selling *them.*"

"Them?"

"Up to it? Everything needs to be put together within two months. Each logo has been budgeted at 4.5k. That keeps the agency sweet."

"For that they could go for butternut or even apple with all the trimmings," Dan said enthusiastically.

"Fine. The thing is, make sure that they are solid and stylish."

"'Stylish' and 'giant thunderbolts' carved out of wood aren't really terms I would put together."

"And the profit margin – how does that sound?" Amy asked.

"Enough for me to treat you to Bestival tickets."

"Why, thank you sir…" Amy said, beaming.

"Mind you," considered Dan, as he crunched then chomped into a piece of battered cod, "there's always maple or lime…"

Amy grinned. Dan was his old self. She had missed him.

Chapter 2

I T CREPT UP ON him. Sam had become a mindless junkie. He was nowhere without the in-built Satnav. Luckily, if he took the occasional wrong turn, the guide patiently re-routed him. The Satnav's arrows had done a reassuring job. Kate Bush's album, 'Fifty Names for Snow', was relaxing. Time passed quickly. Familiar crackle of cobbles beneath the XK-S Coupe's Pirelli tyres set off Sam's deeper Pavlovian conditioning instincts. He was almost home.

Kate Bush's mild as a dove, gentle voice drifted through the custom fitted, Bowers & Wilkins speakers. "… You've got forty-four to go" she sang, counting the 50 names. By the time Kate reached '32', Sam had bought the supercharged 5.0 litre V8 to a stop. He finally switched off the music, pruning the forty-ninth word in two.

Sam was about to step out when a call came through.

"Y'hello," Sam answered.

"Hi Sam, Geraldine Silver," replied the voice.

"Hey Gerry. We should stop meeting like this. It's only been a couple of days. People are going to talk!" Sam joked. "Any updates?"

"Eleven days to be precise. The paperwork's finally back. I thought we could go through it," replied Geraldine in her familiar unruffled voice.

"Um, for sure," replied Sam tentatively. He reached over to the iPad on the passenger seat to check his iCal appointments from 'M'. "Shall I pop down tomorrow? First thing looks good."

"Ten at mine?" asked Geraldine.

"Have you finally made heads and tails of everything?" asked Sam.

"We can talk," Geraldine replied.

Sam spotted a faint smudge on his Piel Frama iPad cover.

"The queen of particulars," Sam countered with a trace of edginess in his voice.

"As your monarch, you better," Geraldine said. "Send my love to Liz. We'll catch up first thing."

"Will do – I need a top up," Sam said, growing increasingly irritated by the smudge.

"Maybe. Let's get together in the morning," Geraldine replied.

The Bowers & Wilkins shuffled its music. It picked up 'Lux Aeterna'.

Sam rubbed at the mark on the iPad cover. Polish might do the trick, he considered. With that he stepped out of his 'carcoon' and, with a duty free bag carrying the Chanel in one hand and fluffy rabbit in the other, he walked the final few steps towards sanity.

Liz and Mia were watching the catch-up of *Eastenders* on the Bio Vision TV.

"Hey people!" Sam called, cutting into a Walford café waitress' chirpy spiel.

"Dad. You're home!" squealed Mia.

"Living, breathing and bringing along a special someone," Sam replied, introducing the knee-high rabbit with arm-length floppy ears.

Pushing the ringer on her right around with her thumb, Liz glanced at the cotton-tailed toy.

"Are you ever going to learn that our daughter is long-past being a baby?" teased Liz.

"I know, I know. But just take a look at this fella's face…"

Mia grabbed the huggable bunny. Given that she was totally nowhere near any boys from school, club or Skype-cams, she cuddled the rabbit.

Sam leant over the sofa and gently squeezed Liz's shoulders.

"This is for you," he said, handing over the duty free bag containing the Chanel.

"Thanks hon," Liz said, reasoning with herself that maybe, after all, the last No. 19 could do with a top-up.

Following the revelation that one of Walford's oldest cheeky chappies (who's character's audience approval figures were on the decline) was having an affair with the Queen Vic's recovering alcoholic barmaid's son's best friend, who had just been released from prison for dealing in dodgy motors, the Roberts family called it a night.

Sam and Liz's room was one flight up from Mia's bedroom (which, Liz had allowed her to decorate, within reason, in a colour scheme of Mia's own choosing).

The master bedroom took up the entire loft space (which was considerable). A large triple-glazed dome that could only be seen from the back of the property provided a *tour d'horizon* of the sky. Thanks to the mansion being distant enough from streetlights, on a clear night the sphere's window revealed the heaven's rhinestones glittering in spectacular hues of tanzanite, ruby and opal.

Chunky wooden roof beams crisscrossed over a queen-sized bed. To the left and right of the bed, low-standing cabinets each carried DAB radios and nickel-frosted lamps. Doors towards the far right of the bed led to walk-in wardrobes. Further doors in the room led to separate en-suite bathrooms. There was enough space for a rose-red sofa, trouser press and two dressers.

A squared entrance framed inside a three-sided wall of 7.6cm glass crowned with a chrome handrail was sunken into the centre floor of the room. A simple wooden staircase led to the floor below. The rest of the bedroom floor was laid in cast resin flooring that sat on a tailored soundproofed pad.

Sam laid on the right side of the bed, Liz, the left. The frosted lamps shed a hoary shadow across their faces.

"You know, I worry about you," Liz said.

"I'm fine. Really."

"Migraines and stuff?"

"Funny. Gerry rang in the car. I think that after all the proddings and pullings, she's stumbled on a new prescription. I'm seeing her tomorrow."

"You work too hard," Liz said.

Whilst reprimanding his never-ending work schedule, recently Liz had become increasingly restless herself. During the day, there was the boutique and Laura. But, come the nights, even with Mia to fuss about, time and agitation twitched on her hands like Hex Bugs. Too many loose ends cross-stitched through her head.

Maybe she should call Gerry directly about Sam's migraines, Liz wondered, touching her ring? She decided to wait, at least until Sam saw Gerry in the morning.

A pause.

"I was chatting to Laura today about things."

"Things? Is the boutique OK?" asked Sam.

"The 'ladies who lunch' still browse the Carvens and Diane von Furstebergs. But even they are moving with the times. Take this morning: Claudia James – you know – the one who made the fuss about the village square."

"Er…" Sam mumbled.

"It doesn't matter. The thing is, even she – we are talking Claudia

James here – was reading from the new Kindle – Claudia James!"

"The shock is just too much for me to take," Sam replied, nonchalantly.

Despite pouting her lips, Liz enjoyed the chance to gossip and chat about loose ends: catch up and explore common ground.

"Anyway, your guy, Leon Bailey Green, got it right about the discount designer site. Just off-the-peg season fashions at bargain prices. 'Digital relationships'. Laura insists we hang on to the boutique. I am not convinced. The money is in the site. Leon got Persky and Neil Binley to make sure that the augmented reality, 360 degree personalised catwalks work brilliantly. Darren Strom from Vmal sorted out the rest of the webby-wot-nots. We're handling distribution ourselves."

"Augmented reality, eh? From bricks-to-clicks…" Sam said.

"Laura calls it an 'onlet'."

"What?"

"The 'just off the peg' site. You point your mobile at a label and voila – you're watching the catwalk."

"Interesting… could catch on. Want me to run it past the Dot Nerds?"

"Thanks, but I am sure we plain girls can just about muddle through."

The small talk reached a hiatus. A full 79 seconds of silence hung, swaying above their heads. All either could do was just lie and wait for the peace to plummet.

Liz rolled over to close her light and shutdown the iPad on its diminutive Magnus stand.

The room's half-light perfectly picked out shadows.

"I'm trying figure it out," Sam said, at last breaking the stillness. "What do you mean by 'things'?"

"Things, stuff… I don't know. Well I do, but I don't quite, if you see what I mean," replied Liz elusively.

The pendulum began to swing once again.

"Do you love me?" she asked suddenly.

A further eight seconds pause.

"Where is all this coming from?"

"Do you still love me?" Liz repeated, feeling not only awkward, but increasingly anxious by Sam's sluggish comeback.

"It's just the business and travel, the bloody headaches…" Sam said, nestling into the pillow to face Liz. "So come on, what's really going on here? What's happened?"

"Nothing. Truly. It's just that… well, sometimes I guess a girl just needs to know."

"You read too many articles in that *Psychologies* mag of yours."

"Say what you like, but don't diss *Psychologies,* mister," sniggered Liz, with a sneer, covering her disappointment that Sam didn't immediately jump in with some kind of instant reassurance.

"You say I work too much. You worry too much. I love you Mrs Roberts – and you can tell that to anyone who needs to know – on a need-to-know basis. Even Claudia wot-nots."

It took a little longer than she hoped, but eventually, the comfort had arrived.

"Sam," Liz whispered, looking directly into his eyes (just as she had 19 years earlier, standing with a saggy copy of the *Daily Mail* over her head), "I just wanted…"

"… to know," Sam said, finishing her sentence.

He stretched to switch off the lamp. Slipping his left arm underneath and around Liz's waist, he held her close.

"We're OK Mrs Roberts. Or as Mia would say, 'sweet.'"

"And Matt?"

"Ah, the Peter Pan of slang. An anachronism personified. Between you and me, I think that every night he plugs a USB stick into his ears and downloads the latest jargon basement buzzwords."

Liz giggled. Sam followed. "Mind you, I couldn't be without him." Sam added.

As with each night for the previous 239 nights, Liz instinctively rolled back to face her side of the bed. The pair dovetailed. Sam gazed at pictures of tiny marigolds on the collar of Liz's PJs. Liz watched the little circle in the centre of her iPad wilt into the dark.

Each wondered how much, and what the other recognised, believed, assumed, feared... knew? The regrets? The isolation? Boredom? Dejection? Aimlessness? Uncertainty?

Each owned fears. Neither knew which were shared, nor spoke of the knots in their stomachs tied to uncertainties in their heads. Or how the rope pulled tighter, the longer they were apart. It was like having a constant craving to return to where they began 19 years earlier. Tonight, as they lay in wait, the space between them seemed wider. The knotted rope twisted firmer than ever.

"Anachronism personified," Sam repeated, loosening the silence, before taking a long yawn. "He'd definitely say 'awesome'."

"'Sweet'," corrected Liz.

"Good night sweet," Sam whispered, as he unravelled arms and legs to face his empty side of the bed.

"Good night."

Liz looked through the glass dome. A nomadic cloud transformed the moon's snowy light into an opaque grey.

Chapter 3

THE VELVETY EDGE OF the small wooden crucifix besides Geraldine Silver's all-in-one printer lay witness that it had been held many times, but always returned safely to its home. The printer itself was on a Somerton chest of drawers in a corner of the room. Nearby was an adjustable examination couch. A small, wall-mounted LED spot was surrounded by half drawn curtains.

A blood pressure monitor sat on Geraldine's classic double pedestal desk next to a Dell screen. The surgery's wall carried an x-ray light box near a steel-and-glass clinic cabinet. The cabinet contained drawers of potions, swabs, needles and other medical paraphernalia. Opposite, a small two-seat sofa stood in front of the apartment's Victorian sash windows.

The room itself was at the far end of the apartment on level 4a of a property in Montagu Square, central London. Its exterior hadn't changed much since Eleanor Rigby first tucked her face away in a jar kept by the door of a nearby apartment. Visitors to the doctor could either take an elegant Victorian elevator to the fourth floor, or climb its twisting set of stairs covered by a well-trodden Axminster runner.

The apartment door opened to a long corridor. A neatly proportioned, bow-fronted mahogany side cabinet inlaid with satinwood marked the corridor's midpoint. Above, a subtly ornate golden frame held a replica portrait of 'The Veil of Veronica' by Claude Mellan.

Doors lead to… well aside from a sensible WC… Sam still never actually knew. Geraldine handled all her own paperwork. So there was no need for a secretary.

Over the years, get-togethers were held at halfway spots, or his place. Geraldine was single. Although Liz and Laura occasionally invited along someone they considered a good catch, none ever gelled – well at least not as a long-term mould.

Sam sat on a captain's side chair next to Geraldine's desk, the doctor on an embroidered cushion that rested on a leather-bound, high-back swivel chair.

The Dell's screensaver displayed a Jacquie Lawson image called 'Serenity'.

"So, thanks for coming," Geraldine said.

"I managed to park opposite Costa's."

"Great. But, like last time, if you would have shouted, I could have given you a permit."

Sam slapped his head. "Doh!"

"Next time – don't forget."

"Consider myself put in the corner," Sam said.

"I wanted to get all the results through before asking you in. Besides, I knew you were overseas."

"So, what's up this time doc?" Sam asked sassily.

Geraldine rested her left hand over a manila file next to a small white cardboard pillbox. The file was stuffed with paperwork, x-rays and other bureaucracy that made the world of private medicine go round.

"Well, as you know," she continued, "we've run all the usual checks. Plus more."

"More… I know these days the insurance people are thorough, but even by your standards, maybe you over-did it…"

"The good news Sam is that you're OK – for now."

"Now? Is the throbbing going to get worse? I've slowed down the chocolate. I'm drinking the water…"

"That's all good! The thing is the MRI, CT and EEG scans picked up something. I had a gut feeling. That's why I decided on the extra tests."

"*You* decided. Not the insurance people. Where is this heading?" quizzed Sam, noticing Geraldine fiddling with the small crucifix on her necklace.

"You have what appears to be a small, and from what I gather, deeply sited meningioma."

'M-e-n-i-n-g-i-o-m-a'. The word was totally alien, every letter as colossal as a wall that stretched further and higher than any fanciful fences.

For the first time in a very long while Sam felt blank. No brilliant angles popped into his head. No counter measures. No 101 quick get outs. No flim. No flam.

Nothing.

He wasn't sure if he was more stunned by what Gerry said, or that he – Sam – was at a complete loss to know what to think at all.

The pre-migraine prickling; even the dots and flashing lights (which although still there) had calmed considerably since a year earlier. The dots had become part and parcel of what and who Sam was. He despised them, but like people with far worse illnesses than his, accepted them. He had to. What he didn't expect was for the migraines to be a part of what he was going to become.

He sucked in a broad breath. The air streamed through his clenched teeth.

"What is 'mening'– whatever?" he asked.

"Meningioma," Geraldine clarified, letting her hand rest on the file. "OK, to begin with, all the tests so far suggest that it is probably not cancerous."

Sam sighed with relief.

"In fact, ninety per cent of meningiomas turn out benign."

"So what's the plan?"

"At this stage, nothing. We just wait. See what happens – if anything."

"So, it's not a disaster…"

"Put it like this, you are in a kind of sticky spot – but not totally glued. You have what is called an 'a-typical meningioma'."

"A-typical – typical of me," Sam chipped in lackadaisically.

"A-typical meningiomas are neither benign, nor malignant. They are sort of in between. We both know about the memory issue. You haven't been vomiting, or getting any sensations of numbness, have you?"

"I would have said."

"Exactly. Which is why right now, we don't need to be alarmed. For example, no way are we looking at surgery. At least not at this stage."

"This stage?"

Instinctively Geraldine brushed her hand against the crucifix.

"Firstly it is in a part of the brain which is quite deep. Frankly Sam, it's not even worth the risk of inviting unnecessary complications. Especially as, in all likelihood, this will turn out to be benign. Sam, you simply don't have the right combination of symptoms to panic. Secondly, meningiomas usually grow slowly – we are talking really, really, slowly."

"Could I die?" Sam asked, getting to the point, looking directly at Geraldine's brown eyes.

"Yes," Geraldine answered unequivocally, softening her conclusion by adding, "but… it's unlikely, in the short term. Even if in six months or a year it actually turns out to be something… well… more significant, we can look at it."

"Can it be cured?" Sam asked, sensing an imminent tingle.

"Again, ninety per cent of cases turn out benign. Like an annoying spot that pops up in the wrong place."

"But if it isn't just a bloody zit, then what is it? Can it be dealt with?" Sam said angrily, overruling his own unwritten law to stay calm before reaching conclusions.

Geraldine gave him space.

"In all likelihood, yes. Because of its position, surgery wouldn't be an option. But, and it's a fantastic 'but'… there's lots of other treatments open to us."

"Worst case scenario?" Sam ventured.

"We'll stop things progressing any further. You'll live with it – like the migraines (which, by the way, I have a promising new prescription for you to try)."

Geraldine handed Sam a box of foil-sealed pills from her desk.

"Do I tell Liz? What about the business?" asked Sam.

Geraldine took Sam's hands into hers.

"Sam. Come on. Believe me, you are not about to drop dead. I've made some enquiries… in case you needed reassurance. There's a gentleman I know who works at Cedars-Sinai hospital in LA. He's pioneered some exciting work in neurosurgery and treatments. This man is rated as one of the best – if not the best. For the next five weeks he's on the lecture circuit. However, I've pulled some strings. If you want, you can meet him next month. Remember, you – we – are in no rush."

Sam licked his upper lip, briefly resting his tongue on its centre.

The philtrum. The word popped into Geraldine's head from her earliest med student days.

"In terms of Liz," she continued, "speaking as your doctor, it's your decision. But as your friend – and hers – I would say something. As for the business, I think for now we can safely say, 'the shop is still open'."

Sam looked down at Geraldine's cupped hands. His eyes glazed over. A tear, then more, dribbled down his cheek.

"Hey you. Where's all this come from? It's going to turn out fine – honestly," comforted Geraldine.

"I'm sorry," Sam said, drawing his hands away. "It must be shock… Well, this is definitely a new experience." Sam was choked by a sudden smog of confusion and bewilderment. "This isn't me. Or maybe for once, it is… Sorry, Gerry."

Geraldine had seen Sam occasionally lost for words before. However, it was always medically connected with his symptoms. Not this time. She offered a tissue.

"What are you apologising for? You know… you've already achieved so much. Way more than most people could ever dream of. A loving wife, a fantastic daughter… a business empire."

"Yeah, including a golf ball in the head. This is sounding like some kind of eulogy," Sam laughed forlornly as he wiped his nose.

"Rubbish. No one mentioned 'golf balls'. Besides, your journey is only just beginning – there's still a great deal more. You'll see."

Wiping his eyes, Sam gave his old friend a peck on the cheek.

"You're right. I just don't know why, or what, came over me. 'Ninety per cent' you say; I've faced worse odds. Much worse."

"A Birdie. Sam Roberts beat them every time," Geraldine joined in.

"… Well, ninety per cent of the time," Sam conceded.

Geraldine grinned, tenderly adding, "I am always here Sam. Your family is here. Matt — well no one can ever seem to shake him off!"

Between them, the two friends eked out a chuckle.

Sam stood up, ready to move on. Geraldine glanced briefly towards the carpet. She clutched the crucifix, whilst hiding a frown reserved for her and the carpet alone.

She escorted him back through the corridor towards the front door.

Sam paused at the Claude Mellan. "I've never really looked at this thing. It's quite exquisite," he said.

"The original is in the British Museum," replied Geraldine. "See what he did?" she continued, pointing towards the details of the face in the picture. "It's all one continuous line. Sometimes fine, sometimes thicker, a wider space here, a tighter band there, sometimes greater depth; always one uninterrupted line."

Sam studied the picture closer. She was right: the entire picture was drawn with a single spiralling stroke starting at the tip of Jesus' nose.

"Look at the Latin inscription. 'FORMATVS VNICVS VNA'," Geraldine said, nodding towards the foot of the picture. "It's not quite your *Dum Spiro, Spero,* but, in way, it still offers a measure of hope," she continued, feeling quietly satisfied about making the link.

"It means 'the one formed in one'. The story goes that on the way to Golgotha, a woman — St. Veronica — took pity on Christ as he was forced to haul the cross to Calvary. She wasn't afraid of the guards holding back the crowds whilst shoving him onwards."

"Sounds like the riot squad and anti-capitalism protestors," Sam jumped in, beginning to step back into his familiar, safe self.

Geraldine smiled and then continued. "Veronica pushed past the guards and offered Jesus her veil to clean the blood from his forehead.

After taking the chance to wipe his brow, he returned the veil. Later, looking at it, St. Veronica saw that Christ's face had been etched into the cloth."

Geraldine turned towards Sam who was studying the deftness of the artist's work.

"I suppose that's what we all have to do sometimes," she said. "Be there, when people need us along the road."

"The ups, downs, twirls and turns of life eh," replied Sam. "You've always had your faith," he continued, thinking about the crucifix by the printer and her pendant.

"Everyone deserves a little genuine faith," Geraldine said, as they reached the front door.

"I guess they do," Sam agreed, deciding to walk down the winding stairs.

Chapter 4

Despite being bare-footed, the baby of the family stood 2.3m tall. Yet, weighing in at 6000kg and standing 9.144m tall, in terms of size, the decapitated horse's head, just a short trot away, was comfortably first past the post.

Rather than head straight to the Kendal Street car park, Sam felt like taking a short walk to Marble Arch, close to the horse and family's neighbourhood.

He called 'M' on the phone.

"How are you? I don't have anything big on today do I?"

"The morning is free – although you did ask me to put a question mark next to 8 a.m. today or lunchtime tomorrow, ref: calling HK," she replied.

"The Hong Kong business."

"Oh, Matt was in – after Martin's files. He also picked up a couple of others to chase up various account directors."

"Sound's like everything is in hand."

"Coming in later?"

"Not sure yet. I am bit tied up with some stuff. If anything important crops up that Matt can't handle or if you need me, call…"

"… I know, 'International Rescue'," she replied, reciting Sam's time-honoured catchphrase (which was at least more amusing than the James Bond line).

Finishing the call, Sam bought a bottle of Evian from a small kiosk on the Edgware Road. At the traffic lights, he crossed over the Bayswater Road to join the throng of people on the Jelly Babies' patch near the horse.

The colourful babies had joined the UK's propaganda displays in the lead-up to the 2012 Olympics. Further propaganda included 'advising' homeowners whose property could be spotted by TV cameras during races, such as the marathon, on what (and how) to plant in their front gardens.

Back when the Jelly Family sculpture was originally unveiled, its artist, Mauro Perucchetti, explained: "On first glance, they seem very sweet, but from certain angles, they can look slightly sinister, especially on a large scale… They could easily embody the unity of family and the multicultural aspect of modern society that is so prevalent, especially in London and the world today."

The vitreous jelly brood stood with their backs to a discreet memorial at the end of the Edgware Road leading into Bayswater Road. However, you couldn't blame them or any tourists who unintentionally passed by the memorial. It was at the end of a traffic island. Its plaque marked the site of the Tyburn gallows.

Until the late eighteenth century, during public holidays, executions at Tyburn attracted big crowds. These included London apprentices who, on 'dangling days', were given time off. (A subtle reminder of how fortunate they were: carrying, climbing, crawling, constructing and complying just to keep their jobs.)

Considering it was London, the weather was good. Not wanting to risk a migraine, Sam wore his Ray-Bans. A whisp of clouds laced through the azure skies. Adapting his jacket as a ground sheet, Sam sat on the grass bank overlooking the happy family and torsoless horse.

He reached into his Lee jeans pocket for the packet of pills. As with all medications, this prescription came with a neatly folded list of warnings in alphabetical order: *Blood clots – Depression – Diarrhoea – Difficulty sleeping – Eye problems – High blood pressure – Increased appetite – Increased body hair – Irregular periods – Osteoporosis – Skin problems – Stunted growth in children and teenagers – Unusual headaches, with eyesight problems – Water retention – Worsening of diabetes – Worsening of epilepsy.*

It's a toss up between whether the side effects or symptoms kill me first, Sam reflected, analysing the list. Popping two pills, washed down with the Evian, he opted for the side effects.

The nearby park benches were full. Families enjoyed a day out. Tourists took in the sites. Workers shared gossip. The unemployed watched the cars go round the road circling the Arch.

Today, some of the workers were complaining about the "stupid upgraded office system" which, complying with the company's new group owners, required an overseas call to the central tech department simply to get the IT man (five desks away) to look at your computer. Under the new group's efficiencies process system, a direct request for IT assistance would only result in an urgent email to call back the overseas IT Tech Central department, who would inform the IT man to email you. Complying, he would send a short message that he would check the computer, just as soon as he finished going through a batch of high priority emails from… Tech Central.

As the grouchy workers consoled each other, an unemployed man, totally oblivious of their conversation, was turning his mind inside out trying to find a way out and back to work as normal.

Somewhere in the back of their minds, all of them watched

movies of themselves, based on scripts countlessly re-written by a never-ending team of additional contributors.

Elsewhere, a spread of buttocks splayed next to a saddle of Barclays bikes branded their mark in the soft grass.

Sam enjoyed people watching (an old habit). When he was no older than seven, his mother often sat besides him on a bench in Gunnersbury Park, Ealing. It was opposite a lake facing a magnificent shrine. The building featured four Doric columns crowned by a pediment decorated with ox skulls and garlands.

A combination of Sam's active imagination and school lessons on Greek mythology did a Huck Finn and Tom Sawyer; convincing him that the shrine was in fact a temple to Poseidon, who watched over the lake (or as Sam imagined – the 'Great Sea').

Weather permitting, Sam's mother bought cornets ('99s') piled high with swirls of puffy ice cream from the Tony Bell van. Each '99' was spiked with a chocolate Flake. Mum always chomped the stick before licking the cloud. Sam went straight for the ice cream, nudging the Flake with the tip of his tongue to the bottom of the cornet to create a 'Sam-made', chocolate-wafer, gooey delight.

When the leaves on the trees turned from a supple green to bones of twigs, flasks of warm tea replaced the ice creams. By that time, Sam had learnt to recognise the park's regulars' idiosyncrasies.

An old couple, 'dressed to the nines', often ambled along. Usually the lady muttered something to the gentleman, after which, they would come to an abrupt halt.

The gentleman would shake his head. Then, following more words from the lady, nod, before together, they plodded onwards.

There were the girls who skipped, whispered and giggled.

Then, there was a man who always carried a rolled up copy of *The Times* newspaper. Sam often spotted him on a bench, tucked between some trees. Every so often, the man would put his *Times* aside and take out a small brown paper bag from his coat pocket. Tilting his head, the man brought the bag to his lips, then, twiddling with its contents, replaced the bag into the coat, and continued to deliberate the headlines.

Whereas Sam's father certainly taught him how to deal with people, his mother meticulously showed whom he was dealing with.

… Back in Marble Arch's Jelly Babies and horse head terrain, Sam spotted a woman wearing stumpy Ugg desert boots, Brand Religion jeans and a plain black top. She whipped out her CrackBerry and snapped a picture of the nag.

Another young mum pushed her toddler in a pram towards the Jelly Babies family. Lifting the infant, she pointed at the different colours. The youngster squealed with delight. Judging by the toddler's clothes and watching how the mum's glances at passing couples lingered slightly longer than normal, Sam reckoned that she was single. She clearly adored the child. Although unaccompanied, she had a sense of certainty – definitely for the child – and perhaps, Sam thought, about herself.

A courier stood looking at the horse's head. He was dressed in padded leathers, lined and lubricated with years of sweat. His left arm was threaded through his Shoei's visor gap. From his angle it must have looked as if the horse was kissing some sanctified stone. Munching into a Double Cheese Empire Burger, the courier stretched to see the rusted horse's serrated neckline. Then, following another circuit around the polished black stone that supported the nag's head, the courier wiped his hands on the leathers before finishing off his burger.

So it was. People chatted, strolled, ate, read, stared, caressed, imagined, listened or snapped pictures – mostly whilst cruising their tablets and phones.

Squinting at the sun, Sam took another swig of Evian. Even if they lost their jobs, I bet they'd still queue for the latest Mountain Lion upgrades, Sam thought, if only to 'Google Goggles' their locations. He felt a bizarre mix of pride and prejudice, knowing that Steve had made a bigger impact on the world than he could have ever dreamt.

To him, at least the logic seemed to be sound.

Augmented consumerism saved tired arms from heavy shopping bags. However, hours spent hunched over screens were resulting in generations of new variants of Kyphosis as well as neurosis. Pre-frontal lobes (popular with neuromarketers) disconnected. Vertebrae fused.

Surfers who were Vulcan mind-melded to upgraded devices, compulsively swiped barcodes, or fingered image recognition software. OCD (obsessive consumerism disorder) was breaking out. Fastidious rubbing of digits left layers of dead skin on Chinese-perfect scratch-proof screens. The payoff was worth it. Streams of product details were discharged to databases describing millions of similar online goods. Within seconds, the cart adding 'Quasimodos' were showered with seductive offers (excluding postage and packaging), climaxing in pleas and e-coupons to "buy and save now!"

Inflamed landlord rates at high street shops, like the ones just up the road in Oxford Street, as well as Liz's back home, were transforming stores into little more than walk-through showrooms and outlets.

The Oxford Street stores welcomed visitors with a sweet spray of success. Each floor had columns of changing rooms, managed by young assistants. The 'wardrobe advice team' sorted piles of "thanks, but it didn't quite fit" clothes. Simultaneously, they also did their best at herding backlogs of customers with garments (maximum four per person), who waited patiently to see if their bum looked big in a dress or suit.

Independent former blogging consumer experts in everything from photography to fashion (especially those also on the telly or radio) replaced tolerantly persuasive departmental managers.

As the amount of checkout girls and sales staff decreased, the numbers of warehouse forklift truck drivers and delivery despatch vans increased. As did the vacuum of unemployed who were too slow to catch either the truck- or van-driving career bandwagon.

Stifled by boredom, the unwaged vacuum filled up their daily spare space looking at job sites, scanning, swiping and using their idle thumbs and fingers to snap up instant online bargains as treats for surviving their loneliness.

Within 48 hours, a neatly-packed, impulse-bought product would be delivered to their homes. Once the seal was broken and contents discovered to be the wrong order, the otherwise unemployed buyer could occupy the rest of their day returning, via their mobile 'everythings', the wrongly delivered packages.

Sam sniggered. Matt would definitely have approved the logic.

Sam spotted a worker snap an 'early bird'-filtered Instagram of her half-eaten chicken and condiment sandwich. Doubtlessly the picture was already on route to her social page to be admired, along with the thousands of other Tweet and catch-up takeaways that afternoon.

Another family looked in awe at the horse's head. Like years ago in Gunnersbury Park, it occurred to Sam that people made the landscape, rather than empty memorials housing mythical sun-god colossuses or deformed centaurs.

Sam's phone ID rang out 'Something Tells Me' by Herman's Hermits. It was Liz. He didn't have a clue what to say, or how to begin.

Chapter 5

FEELING SOMEWHAT AWKWARD AT her shoulders being gently clutched, Amy swivelled round from studying the upcoming live road show planning schedule. The project was huge and, as well as coordinating an international team, she had to deal with office politics.

"How is it going?" Matt asked.

"All's on track. The e-shots are producing good numbers. The quality of related Tweets and Google+ recommendations have picked up some nice community engagement. Irina Chernikova (she joined from Smart Insights) puts it down to Facebook credits and gamification. It's gone more viral than the 2011 'Free game for playing the game' project. Jim has linked it to a 'JustGiving' page."

"Neat. Who came up with that?" asked Matt.

"Huw Sayer, a bright copywriter. I 'borrowed' him from John Beavis' team."

"Well don't forget to give him back to the maestro at some point," Matt said, jotting Huw's name in his Quo Vadis pocket notebook.

"Dean and the Multiply team are closing loose ends with technical links to Beaverton. Small Fry Films has finalised the storyboard for the intro video. O2's been given the program for the electronic billboards…"

"Are the TV stations playing ball? Do you need me to give another call to Sally at CNN?" Matt asked.

"CNN is linked, as are Fox, ABC and Sky. ITV say's it's going to be tight, but they're on it," Amy said, checking Performa's ever razor-sharp iArticulate business performance software.

"The organic EcoCreeper shirts are in hand. Rix is finalising what's looking like a great line-up. He's confirmed Jeremy Jacobs to keep things on track. He's trying to get hold of LA's top sports coach. And there's an upcoming band, led by newcomer Ben Beuno, who Jolie Lash predicts will be a future Brit Awards winner. Zeus' people are really keen to seal a deal with Ben before anyone else. Plus Rix has confirmed Coloccini and the usual sports and celeb suspects... I've sorted the wooden logos – everything's on schedule," Amy concluded with an assured 'I've got it covered' grin.

"You're cooking..." Matt said, waiting for Amy to complete the slogan.

"Er... yes... simply boiling over with it all," Amy replied, slightly bemused.

Boiling over... Matt thought. "I like it," he announced, tucking his Mont Blanc back into its pocket-sized bed. "I'd like to run an open kimono policy on this. I've asked Pete to pitch in – just in case anything gets 'hosepiped'. This project must head true north. That OK with you?"

"Sure," Amy answered, rubbing the back of her ear.

Catching her line of sight, Pete waved his right hand. Amy smiled and returned the gesture, hoping her wave back didn't mirror her guarded scepticism.

"OK then. Great, let's keep close," Matt said. "Text or email me whenever. Let's corner off some regular all-hands time to go over the progress reports I've checked with Pete. How does Tuesdays and Fridays – first thing, 8.30 – sound? Muffins with Cap."

"Fine," Amy agreed, softly grinding her teeth. Apart from being monitored like some chav wearing a pair of chastity fetters around her ankles, Matt's linguistic gymnastics were getting on her nerves. Most of all, she was peeved that Pete had managed to get fast-bowled in from nowhere.

"Deal done," Matt concluded.

With that, asking his iPhone's Siri to switch appointments, he set off on his morning rounds of guerrilla macro-management.

Good old Matt. Definitely eccentric, always everyone's ultimate life jacket.

In truth, tucked behind the sea of lingo, Matt often felt uncomfortably vulnerable. Apart from perhaps Sam, nobody suspected that, along with market highs and lows, private wins and losses, public respect and reject, family ties and cuts, Matt's sense of precariousness fluxed from full exposure to teetering on total reassurance 'shut-down'.

He hated the whole supervision by tweezers thing. Being a 'Scrum Manager' went against his natural impulse to remain hands off. But there was too much at stake on this one. Besides, he reasoned, maybe Sam's Bell model was right after all. These days, yoghurts were more proactive than certain employees. Add client whims and wants… and Matt didn't have much choice. Neither did any of them, including Sam, whom Matt was convinced felt the squeeze more than he was actually letting on.

At times, in the race for business, simply to maintain momentum, life felt like it was on a treadmill, set at double speed. For the staff, the pace was unforgiving. As leaders, Sam and Matt coped stoically in their own ways. Most of the time, client bureaucracy orchestrated by auditors made projects (or, in the language of brave new words – 'sprints') feel as if they were on the road to nowhere. One misplaced judgement and everything could collapse.

Slipping on a new jacket of optimism and adding another word to his 'connect and coax' vocabulary, Matt left to sort out the yoghurts from the soured milks.

Amy meanwhile returned to her spreadsheets. This time, rather than study them, her eyes glazed over.

Carrying a peace offering of a small teddy bear wearing a miniature T-shirt that featured a client's fabric softener logo, Pete stealthily approached Amy's desk.

"For you," he said, waking Amy from her trance.

"Last of the big spenders eh?"

"Sorry, I couldn't quite get to Harrods in time."

Amy smiled. (Perhaps Pete wasn't a total tosser after all.)

"Looks like we're in this together. Might as well start as we mean to go on," she announced, sitting the bear next to a framed picture of Dan.

"Cool!" Pete replied. "Trust me, I am not about to step on anyone's toes. I reckon Matt must have figured that seeing my last campaign is mostly put to bed, and given the pressure, I might as well get my lot to pitch in. They have the capacity… all under your wings of course."

Ever cautious, Amy nodded. "How about putting everyone together for a confab at 6.30 tonight?" she suggested, fully knowing that the time-slot would cause maximum problems.

"Done deal," Pete said cheerfully.

Amy's Siemens rang.

"Sorry… got to take this…" Amy said, cupping the voice piece.

"No probs. I'll catch you later."

"Guess where I am standing right now," Dan shouted down his HTC.

"Somewhere noisy!" Amy replied.

"One of my top suppliers. I am staring at some stunning examples of Quercus Rubra timber. These are beauties. I would say they're about 11 metres long... Dave just shouted 106.68 centimetres wide. I would say, around 12 centimetres deep."

"One hundred and six point sixty-eight hey! Tell Dave he needs to get a life," Amy replied, resigned to the sad truth that, in the name of either their profession or at least something to occupy their hands, men would always love flimflam.

"With the right staining – not too much mind – I think we have our centrepieces."

"Great. But warn Dave that he'd better have a big truck."

Dan laughed.

Replacing the handset, Amy wondered what a Quercus Rubra actually was in the first place? Whatever it was, it made Dan happy. She returned to contemplating the agonizing prospect of working with Pete's team. Her biggest fear was that more hands on deck would turn out like an *Australian MasterChef* final: too many critics and not enough cooks.

The teddy bear's tiny 'T' was cute. Back on top of things, she summoned Google to search for what she assumed Dan had said. In return, her screen displayed a picture of a bottle of wine called 'Red Ass Rhubarb'. Apparently, it contained 10 per cent raspberries and 90 per cent rhubarb.

Given the bottle's dimensions, Amy concluded it probably wasn't what Dave and Dan had in mind.

Chapter 6

A PRETTY BONICA MEILLAND STOOD in a large ceramic Spanish pot by the boutique's entrance. Suspended above the door was a softly coloured lilac sign, hand painted in a dark mauve Cochin font that read: Camera Della Moda.

The boutique's exterior was painted in a gentle pink and whisper white. A large window revealed two classical mannequins. One dressed in a pretty Carven, the other, a DVF (Diane von Furstenberg). The uncluttered window tempted passing inquisitive shoppers to scan the boutique's generous white space, bordered by polished silver rails with wooden hangers that shouldered rows of designer labels.

Orthodox French wall mirrors divided sections of the boutique into distinctive fashion ranges. There were dresses by Roland Mouret, Giambattista Valli, the obligatory Coco C, and for the austerity conscious, Alice Olivia.

The heart of the boutique had a black oval table with curvilinearly legs. A Waterford crystal bowl, carrying freshly cut rose buds floating on a pool of water, crowned its centre. Two wooden chairs styled in a classic Florentine design stood at each end of the table.

At the rear of the boutique, a Japanese *shoji* opened to a changing room. Inside a large Cheval mirror hung above a padded French Vanity seat. A Louis XVI styled side table carried a silver framed

15.2x10.2cm black-and-white photograph of Gabrielle Bonheur. The lower part of the frame was engraved with her words: "It is always better to be slightly underdressed."

Liz's Rado watch showed 5.45 p.m. Laura had gone. Liz was alone with her iPad.

Two hours earlier, totally pre-occupied with a mission planned the previous night, Laura had left to track down fruit compote for an orange chiffon cake recipe. It was demonstrated the night before on BBC2 by a cockney chef. The dish, especially the one on the plate, looked totally scrumptious.

Good old dependable, blithe-spirited, Laura Stephanie Jones-Robinson lived in an amply apportioned cottage with Michael, her husband for 22 "wonderful years". Both were regularly invited to church events, Rotary Club dinners and local fetes.

Michael ran a fifteen-person strong accountancy practice. He was the younger brother of Thomas, a successful economist based in Europe. Laura always became excited whenever she saw Michael's brother on BBC News. He occasionally popped up on TV with stark warnings to fellow bankers about their dubious practices.

And Michael had won bronze for his parsnips – two years in a row!

During the first part of the 22 years Laura had three miscarriages. The last procedure took her fertility. She hated herself for this, and yet not even Liz suspected it.

Laura had tried all the diet plans. She had already given away an entire wardrobe to the local charity shop and always kept up with the latest diet sensation. In spite of everything, 'Laura' (the one inside her head) never let 'Laura' (the one too often stood alone outside Waitrose) have what she needed. Every effort was sabotaged. Laura deserved nothing less, and craved for much more.

Checking the time again, Liz twiddled with her index finger ring. When that didn't work, she swiped aimlessly through the Elle Collections App.

5.53 p.m. The plan wasn't working.

At 5.58 p.m. Sam switched off the XK. Within a minute, he was outside Camera Della Moda.

Through the window, he could see Liz pre-occupied with her iPad. Sam paused and glanced towards the right of the shop's doorframe. Just over half way up was a mezuzah hewn from Jerusalem stone. It contained a scrolled parchment with 713 tiny Hebrew letters over 22 lines. The words recorded passages from the Torah (the Five Books of Moses): 'Deuteronomy' 6:4-9 and 11:13.

For luck, Buddhists placed *Hotei* gods on shelves. Muslims carried *Hamzahs.* Hindus placed the Swastika over doorways. Sikhs dangled the *Khanda* from rear view mirrors. Atheists and agnostics took their chances with furry dice. The rest placed their hope in lucky zodiacs and confidence in sending their children to Oxbridge.

For Sam, providence was something to be experienced, rather than conjured. Yet, even he had mezuzahs placed on every door in the house (except the toilet). He ensured a mezuzah was on his private office door in Charlotte Street, as well as the entrances of every Barnes and Roberts building.

His parents, like generations before them, followed the tradition as directed by the passages contained in the mezuzah itself.

Annually, during late September or early October – which, according to the Jewish calendar, heralded the final weeks leading up to the Jewish New Year (Rosh Hashanah) and Day of Atonement (Yom Kippur) – Sam's parents took him to Hoop Lane cemetery. Respects were paid to departed family members. (He never mentioned these outings to school friends. They would have freaked out.)

Jewish custom wasn't to lay flowers on graves. Instead, pebbles placed on the cold stones represented surviving close family members. In a way, the mezuzahs reminded Sam of his dad arranging those pebbles.

In keeping with his customary counsel for most occasions, once the pebbles formed a circle, his father, turning to Sam, would mutter, "You think you're in charge, kid. But He's given you the breaks to have it that way. Just when you realise you're not in charge, well, that's when He's given you the chance to get a grip and take charge."

"Yes Dad, whatever…" Sam would answer, itching to just get back home.

Usually, along with blustery autumn showers, a quorum of ten men aged over 13 years old (a Minyan) could be put together from various families who also came to remember loved ones.

Standing amongst them, his father would recite Kaddish, the mourner's prayer. It was a petition for a messianic kingdom to be established within the reader's lifetime. Rather than dwell on death, the prayer affirmed life's blessings through seraphic grace, and requested peace to all.

On leaving the cemetery, the family had a custom of each plucking a leaf from one of the trees at the grounds. Once out and back in the car, each person released his or her leaf out of the window. As the leaves drifted back, individually people would whisper the word, "Mehilla" ("forgive me"). A last token chance to say what they never could whilst the relative was alive.

Every year, Sam still visited the cemetery. He attended synagogue whenever schedules, commitments, flights or an infinite compendium of social and digital distractions permitted (which wasn't that often).

In addition to the mezuzahs, discernible signs of his faith included a menorah — a nine-branched candelabrum used on the

Jewish holiday of Hanukkah. It stood on the Boca do Lobo table.

Then there was the zip-up velvet pouch containing his father's prayer shawl (tallit). Tucked in a drawer, between fragments of memory, was also the tefillin: a set of small, black leather boxes containing scrolls of parchment inscribed with verses from 'Deuteronomy' 6:4-9, 'Deuteronomy' 6:8-11:13-21 and 'Exodus' 13:1-10/13:11-16.

Sam had a copy of his culture's roots – the Torah – in his bookcase. (Muslims displayed the holy Koran; Christians, the King James' Bible. Hindus had a wider a choice, including the *Laws of Manu* and the *Upanishads*. Atheists had a combination of Hans Christian Andersen, Dawkins, and a BBC DVD of Life. Agnostics had all three.)

Each of the Roberts' Five Books of Moses featured commentary by a sage called Maimonides. Besides the set, Sam had a daily prayer book, presented at his Bar Mitzvah (coming of age), and a collection of specially leather-bound prayer books for use on religious holidays. Every year, he only used one – the heaviest. And even that was just on one day: the Day of Atonement. For any other occasional synagogue visits, Sam would use the books provided at the venue.

The collection was actually a 21st birthday gift from his uncle Maurice, his mother's brother. The boxed set was typical of his uncle's generosity (who, like Sam's own father, was a great teller of stories). That said, at the time, Sam would have much more preferred a record voucher from Our Price music. But he couldn't deny that the volumes looked impressive.

There was one other seldom-spotted clue to Sam's background: his grandfather's kippah (a small head covering shaped similarly to the papal Pileolus). Sam kept the kippah in his pocket. Seeing it in the open was as rare as spotting a Pinta Island Tortoise. Sam wasn't quite sure why he carried it. Maybe, along with the mezuzahs, it instinctively gave him a sense of simply 'being' and belonging.

Recalling Gerry's words, "Sam Roberts beats them every time," he stepped into the boutique.

Having flipped over the hand-painted door sign which read, *Closed – but there's always tomorrow!* Mr Roberts walked over to kiss his wife's forehead.

Chapter 7

Wʜᴀᴛ ᴛʜᴇ ᴘᴇɴsɪᴠᴇ ɢʟᴀʀᴇ left out, Liz's fidgeting with her ring filled in.

"I spoke to Gerry."

"So much for client confidentiality."

"None of this seems right. Gerry's been maddening. She barely gave any detail. In the meantime I am just sat here, enduring Laura babbling over her third Gold Blend of the day, going on about who knows what and heaven knows why."

"Maybe she likes your coffee?" Sam suggested impulsively.

The suggestion didn't stir well.

Liz closed the tablet's cover and took a deep breath.

"So, from what you've said so far, this is not a life or death, right?"

"Here I am in the flesh. 'Sam Roberts has not left, nor intends to leave, the building'. In fact, on the drive down I was thinking, its here with you, more than anywhere or anyone else (apart from Mia), that I want to be."

"Do I detect guilt? You've had a sudden career need to run the shop?" Liz snapped, as her thumb once more reached instinctively for the ring. "So there *is* something you are not telling me."

"'No' to everything: I don't want to run the shop. No... I mean, yes, it's not a big deal. A wake-up call, that's all. Take things easier.

Really – that's it. (No Walford market dramatics.) Besides, I've been cooking up this plan for some time now…"

"Plan?"

"An adventure for Mia, you and me."

"Adventure. Samuel, the truth. Seriously now. I'll find out. Is there another woman?"

Sam sighed.

"Just ring Gerry if you like. Here, do it now," he said, tossing his phone to Liz.

"OK, OK! Hold back. I believe you. It's me. Sorry, I panic."

"You'll call her anyway," Sam presumed.

"You know your customers," Liz replied, managing a diminutive grin.

Sam pulled up the chair opposite Liz.

"The bottom line is…"

"Bottom line…" Liz repeated.

"… is… Gerry mentioned it could perhaps, at some point, develop into something more tangible."

Liz stopped twirling the ring.

"Then again," Sam quickly picked up, "so could government manifestos."

Liz neither weakened, nor put aside Sam overlooking her mention of another woman. But that issue, she decided, would be filed away for another time.

"Gerry reassured me that there's no call for surgery, just on-going check ups. Plus there's this different prescription for the headaches: all of which she will confirm."

Liz looked at the carton of pills, then Sam's eyes. Damned poker face, she thought, as she covered her mouth with the palm of her hand, whilst attempting to balance it all out.

"Adventure," she at last said. "You want more time with us? What I really don't get is that's we've been asking you to do for ages."

"Better late than never. We've got the villa. We don't go often enough, I realise that. Thing is, who cares how we got there, but here we are."

"So we just swan off in the middle of what is clearly the worst downturn since whenever it was, that whoever it was on Radio 4 said it was. What about Mia?"

"We'll tell her the truth: we're taking a vacation. Totally. That's the general idea."

Frustration, confusion, irritation and suspicion closed in around Liz's head. The mounting sludge of pending questions and unnerving considerations threatened to conspire into a cataclysmic mudslide.

Sam walked over to the clothes. His fingers traced the corner of an O'Hara wool-crepe Roland Mouret dress.

"How's the shop doing?" he asked in an attempt to smooth the razor-sharp atmosphere.

"Surprisingly, the same as when we spoke last night," Liz snapped back.

Rather than take the bait, Sam continued to inspect the collection.

Liz could feel the mud welling up. Yet, having lived with the man for approaching 20 years, next to Martha and Matt (The M&Ms), she was still the oldest, and definitely the most tolerant, pupil from the Sam Roberts School of Steadfastness.

Despite the potential avalanche still quivering on the precipice, Liz intuitively adopted the classic Barnes and Roberts' crisis management steps that she had seen too many times to mention:

Notify stakeholders (directly).

Acknowledge, but don't automatically admit, fault.

Investigate, listen and collaborate.
Face the truth.
Communicate and cooperate with total transparency.
Tell the truth.
If possible, fix the problem.
Reassure through measurable actions.
Engage with allies.
Learn and improve.
Remain calm and carry on.

Liz continued watching Sam study the dresses – as if he had some deep authoritative knowledge of women's fashion labels. She continued staring at his fiddling until the land settled and her breathing slowed.

"I am sorry," she said finally.

"This is getting us nowhere," Sam added, happy to be released from tedious texture touching.

"Does Matt know?"

"What with the Brand Fish project, a big launch around the corner, and countless other stuff, I haven't bought it up; at least in detail. I understand him. He's full. Besides, I know, he knows and you know the headaches are probably down to stress. I also know you're worried. Me too, but we've been through way more than this. I think, I know, I – we – can handle it. But you need to be there with me."

'Be there'. A myriad of images flashed through Liz's mind at least at the speed of neutrinos – if not tachyons.

'Being there' meant waiting: for the phone call, Skype, kettle to boil, rain to stop, customer to buy, Mia to return, Sam to listen, love to share.

'Being there' was driving her mobile pressure capsule, insulated by a 14 speaker surround sound system that played Cockney Rebel and Steve Harley in the morning, but Dan Hill and Richard Marx at night.

'Being there' was attending B&R's clients' annual flood/ earthquake/drought/hurricane/tsunami benefits – any one of the charitable quintet was acceptable. Each had been carefully chosen by focus groups to be causes relating to the hand of nature, rather than the trigger-happy finger of any radical. Liz donated fashionable outfits to be worn by the affluent and aspirant. (The former being tight fisted, the latter bare knuckled and punching above their weight.)

'Being there' was watching Matt and Sam look as if they owned the world, or emerging from a long talk in the kitchen to glare into empty space and promise each other to pick things up again in the morning.

'Being there' was sitting on a school plastic chair next to Mick and Adele Sopher, Paul and Corinne Miller, David and Katie Leach, Robert and Elaine Vaughan, and still more rows full of Mrs and Mrs, or Ex's and Ms's. Snapping a picture of Mia collecting her music certificate. Beaming at her daughter, whilst feeling totally isolated in an echoing school hall, packed to its bare walls with proud parents.

'Being there' was listening to a coiffured Laura convince herself that England was still in the 1990s. It was accepting that naughty school children were now called 'challenging' and six year olds demanded teachers, friends and the world should stay out of their 'personal space'.

'Being there' was abiding TV news with the family. Listening to a disconsolate commentator explain why pensioners may no longer be able to afford to eat cat food, let alone be cared for.

… Watching a political correspondent reveal that local councils are increasing taxes on… well, just about everything.

… Learning that university graduates are set to become the most educated unemployed and debt-bound generation ever.

… Listening to a well-known Dean who, speaking as softly as a church mouse, explained why he had no other choice than to let a priest go. After all, the priest had claimed that no less than the Saviour could be amongst the anti-capitalist protestors camped outside St. Paul's Cathedral. Liz watched as the Dean struggled to be heard against the crowd that thrust posters of their martyr: Dorli Rainey, an 84-year-old Seattle activist, who had been doused in pepper spray. The Dean concluded, "We felt he needed to pursue his completeness, unconstrained by continued employment. Our prayers go with him."

… Giggling with the family over the news that virtual monkeys randomly striking keys on computer-generated typewriters had managed to recreate the complete works of Shakespeare.

'Being there' was reassuring Mia that, just as every pot has a lid, so love eventually comes to all.

'Being there' was, laughing, crying, arguing, brooding… getting through stretches when she sensed Sam wasn't wholly there and neither was she.

'Being there' was loitering outside the Oxford Street Ecco shoe store, waiting to spot the 'blue baseball cap' whose Hotmail message suggested a get-together at 2.30 p.m. beneath the Selfridges clock. Then, by 2.40 p.m., having thought about 19 years of ups downs, ins and outs… and Mia… dismissing the whole crazy, completely stupid idea… Blending back into the crowds. Leaving the cap to tilt and turn for a further 45 minutes, before he finally headed off to The Marlborough Head pub in North Audley Street.

'Being there' was listening to Sam slither downstairs to pour a full Riedel Crystal glass of Yamazaki whiskey whilst going over the figures again, and still again. Two hours later, discovering him asleep on the table, besides a sheet of management names with question marks drawn, scratched and redrawn, alongside each Pam, Dick or Harry. Gently lifting his head from the kitchen table and onto a pillow. Returning to gently wake him before Mia and breakfast mayhem, in time for a meeting which 'M' reminded her to remind him about…

'Being there' was everything she wished to forget, and the one thing she longed to be.

"We'll muddle through. I'm here, always will be." Liz said, brushing her hand against Sam's arm.

Then and there, Sam felt safe. It was the kind of contained security that any passing driftwood of desire could never remain stable enough to support or sustain.

"So, about Mia…" he ventured.

"Listen mister," Liz said, drawing on determined encouragement, "you believe it's going to be OK. I believe you. Mind you, Mia's got enough on at the moment; what with school and the usual teenage woes."

War, famine, captivity, bankruptcies, homelessness, cutbacks, despondency, illness, seclusion, overdosed kings and queens of pop… irrespective of whatever else was going on in the world, exam worries and teenage angst would always need handling with care. Liz was the best in the world to handle it. That thought was somehow encouraging.

"You're right. But I still like the idea of doing something as a family. Soon, Mia will be too old to hang out with her mum and dad."

"She has mock exams coming up. How about after that?" Liz offered, in search of a compromise.

"Sounds like a plan. Pull your web expedition boots on. Bing 'fun' – five star recommendations only."

Then, for the second time in an hour, whose minutes had been delayed by years, Sam kissed the one person who remained by his side in rain and, maybe once more, in shine.

Chapter 8

Back in 2001 you would have been forgiven for assuming the man walking down Duke Street St. James was none other than James Bigglesworth himself. The detail that clinched it was the neatly tied silk cravat, and short, well-kept handlebar mustachio. However, Bigglesworth was fictional. This man clearly wasn't.

Even if for some fanciful reason you still believed it was Bigglesworth (nicknamed 'Biggles'), should you have been of a certain age, you would have known that the 'real' Biggles didn't actually sport a moustache, nor regularly wore a cravat.

However, like Biggles, Bristol-born Alexander Weight enjoyed nothing better than piloting airplanes. (The original Biggles flew Sopwith Camels during World War I, Hawker Hurricanes and Supermarine Spitfires in World War II, and later Hawker Hunter jet fighters.)

Alex had shares in a couple of light aircrafts. He was a leading international corporate attorney. Like Biggles, Alex spoke several languages. Equally, there was a genuine sense of professionalism and chivalry about him.

His sharp legal brain, along with the skill to address international audiences in fluent Italian, Mandarin and French, led to a career working at the most senior level for some of the world's most prestigious law firms. By 2012, in solidarity with global cut backs, Alex had shaved the moustache, taking years from his appearance whilst veiling decades of experience.

Sam had known him since the Duke Street days. Alex was a partner at CBA Legal. Initially he handled M&As for R&B's flourishing communications group. As the agency expanded, so he was called on to deal with problems ranging from employment issues to international tax regulations.

As each situation presented itself, so Alex directly advised Sam or Matt. His phone calls to the right people to get legislative projects sorted on time, in budget, and with the minimum risk of uninvited public or competitor meddling, were legendary.

Should a smooth legal strategy be needed by one of Sam's US companies, Alex recommended Gary Ruvio, one of the Big Apple's leading attorneys for such cases. From litigious slurs to last will and testaments, Alex remained by Sam and Matt's side.

Sam checked the time: 1.15 p.m. He was already 15 minutes late, but decided to give Skype a shot anyway.

A white tick spat through Alex's green Skype glob. Sam clicked the video call button. Within seconds, Alex was online. Sam could just about make out the skyscrapers silhouetted through Alex's office window, behind his desk. Each tower competed tit-for-tat – metre for metre – for supremacy of the Hong Kong skyline.

"Hey Sam, how are you today?"

"Never better. I meant to get in touch yesterday but got caught up with stuff."

"Same old…"

"… Same old."

"I needed to talk about some developments here in the Asian market," Alex continued. "Since the tsunamis and Fukushima back in

2011, Japan's never been quite the same. Sure, their officials are always happy to line up for the *hara-kiri* bit, but more than earthquakes alone, regional politics has made the market as uncertain as Italy, Ireland, Portugal or a Monetary Policy Committee's economic forecast."

"So tell me something new. Since Berlusconi became ravioli, the global diet has gone all Twiggy. Pizzas, stews and baklava, fish and chips, burgers, tapas, fries… it's all slimmed down mush."

"Good job I just had lunch," Alex laughed, enjoying the banter. "Bottom line: instability has led to different approaches to either keeping money or making it. The Asian sector is on the up: sharper every day. Patent law and copyright suits are more frequent. Standard essential patents mean crazy royalty payments. The firm has become the best FRAND clients have."

"FRAND?"

"Sorry – 'Fair, Reasonable and Non-Discriminatory'. Thing is, I had a meeting with Martin from the Shanghai agency office. (He was in Hong Kong for the ICEMM conference.) A quarter of his key clients are cutting even further back on ad spend – including online."

"Again, Al – what's new?"

"Big players, especially in IT, get bigger ROI from suing everyone and anyone for patent copying. The future is about who owns software, hardware and cloudware rights."

"Without marketing, it would all be somewhere over the rainbow. Besides, if a software system belongs to one company, why should competitors be allowed to claim it?" Sam said.

"C'mon. What about counterfeit fashion? It's nothing new," added Alex.

"If everyone makes similar-looking cornflakes, before you know it, the only gold-standard difference becomes cost. Quality lands a bronze."

"Hey, I'm a law man, not an ad man. I can tell you this, though: the fight between IT players who one minute are contracted to supply components and software, and the next are sued for making the damn component which the other one asked the first one to supply in the first place, is as merciless as it is convoluted. Take the Taiwanese cloud market – although I am not mentioning any client names…"

"Obviously not," Sam said.

Alex continued. "The original design manufacturers supply bare-bones servers to European and American hardware giants. The brand giants add flesh to it all later. Now, some of the web big players are cutting out the hardware brand names, too. They are going straight to middle men – The ODMs. The Taiwanese are more than happy to make a buck shipping cheap servers for data centres. Goodbye traditional Uncle Sam server makers."

"Yeah well, I don't know if you heard, but mercy's a treasured commodity, sheriff. Once people know where to get some, they'll be knocking on doors. That, my friend, takes marketing."

Alex shrugged.

"Speaking of ROI," Sam continued, "with all due respect, why didn't Martin come straight to me on this?"

"Well…"

"Ah, and here enters the punch line…"

"… This all cropped up because of something else on the boil. I briefed Matt on it a few days ago."

"'M' mentioned Matt's dealing with some files. I just haven't fully caught up yet. No 'International Rescue' calls, so I assumed all was ticking over nicely."

"Would you prefer to talk to Matt directly, or can I bring you up to speed?"

"You know the score with Matt: two heads, one solution, no secrets."

"Maybe that's the secret to a good marriage? Yours is the only business partnership agreement that I have never had to dissolve," said Alex.

"Ant and Dec, Marks and Spencer: as strong as the rock of Gibraltar," replied Sam.

(Alex pictured Laurel and Hardy shaking hands with Wilbur and Orville Wright.)

"OK. Firstly, places like Brazil are catching up with Asia as powerhouses," explained Alex. "They can produce virtually anything cheaper, with just the same quality as the very best."

"Half of the top British brand names are made overseas. The list is as long as a non-disclosure agreement," Sam chipped in.

"Maybe, but now the official Chinese advertising body is drawing up a different kind of agreement that's been kept hush-hush. Local agencies are linking with the UK and US to provide what is being called a 'test bed' for future global launches. Problem is, that unless one of your companies gets on the official list, you're not in – if you see what I mean."

"Can we contest it?"

"They have every legal right to trade with whomever they wish. Martin is jumpy. He is nervous that for the sake of global business and local politics, regional international clients coming out of contracts could switch to 'tick-box' suppliers. I am trying to get hold of the fine print."

"Can't we just buy our way into this thing?"

Alex shook his head. "Obviously I'll ignore that."

"… Obviously," Sam added.

Alex continued, "You've heard me say it many times… legally

speaking one of the first things any Corp needs is a possible exit strategy. At least be prepared in case some other guy tries to push the company through the nearest exit door. First things end up last thoughts. Besides, these days the only pockets deep enough to either save or sway at this global level belong to the European Union and the International Monetary Fund."

"As long as the creditors aren't from Athens."

Sam checked the FT site.

"The Chinese are brilliant capitalists. The old mantra to stay in the black is moving into the red," Alex ventured.

"Got it!" Sam said.

Alex was pleased that whilst neither the FRAND nor Athens gag had clicked, the Chinese one worked.

"… According to analysts, the 'Made in China' label alone brings in a surplus of $540 million dollars a day," Sam pressed on.

Alex nodded gravely, reconsidering his comedic abilities after all.

Sam continued to scan the FT. "China has $3.2 trillion in foreign reserves. By 2011, they'd ploughed in at least $800bn into Euros."

"Good news, though. Brand Fish isn't totally out of its depths yet," Alex added. "Martin said the project is keeping the remaining big names in the Asian region relatively happy."

Sam raised his eyebrows. "Relatively?"

"The official new plan looks like it will adopt charitable aspects of Brand Fish. It'll incorporate good causes promoted by agencies within the state approved list. Share, but on an even bigger scale than your fish concept (if you don't mind the pun)."

"So much for good news. They should call their project 'Brand Shark'."

"The recession is the season for big fish to get swallowed by bigger fish. Us lawyers are left with giving up weekends checking contracts."

"My heart and their wallets bleed for you," Sam quipped.

Alex laughed.

"Yens buy deeper access to the Euro zone market. (See now why ownership is everything?) Whilst the trademark 'Brand Fish' is covered, not even I can stop others donating whatever they wish, however they want, to whomever they like. If anything, once you get China behind such a scheme, their sheer power and ingenuity alone guarantees success for any chosen charities. It's a good thing. The big nurture the growing. Anyway, apart from any ethical issues, trying to intervene would be commercial suicide."

Sam sighed. Becoming increasingly sensitive of his screen's brightness, he massaged his temple.

"Martin is wondering if this could spell the start of something even bigger," Alex continued. "Namely other governments getting in with chosen brand bed-partners looking to push their cred via the charity concept."

"I still don't get why people like Ben didn't pick up on this," Sam jumped back, slapping his palm on the desk in frustration.

"Few knew. Martin suggested I check the legal chatter in other world regions. Assuming that's fine with you."

"I'd expect it," Sam replied. "I still think that if every government jumps onto similar 'brand-wagons' – purely as a PR exercise – you'll end up with even more consumer indifference. Forget 'Chuggers', start thinking 'Bruggers'. One compassionate brand-sponsored lapel pin will look like every other. It's no secret that politicians and business scratch each other's balls: but in private."

Alex took the point and liked the Bruggers quip.

Sam was still angry. "If consumers are expected to support say, health or education, simply because the State can't, then you can add indignation to indifference. Who can blame them? A national lottery for good causes is one thing. I love a TV charity all-nighter. But a separate brand lottery for each government department doesn't work. Even if we align every charity brand with different consumer profiles, the whole thing dilutes the power of the original concept. Besides, what's next: government approved hamburgers sponsoring obesity units? Forget old-style capitalism or communism, Al, Neo-liberalism will slowly turn poor NHS hospitals into rich, administration approved investments."

"Since when have you been such a Lefty? More private money; more advertising spend. (See, I learnt that one from you.) Good for profits." Alex suggested.

"Well at least I taught someone something. The thing is, which side's going to pay for the loss of integrity?"

Despite the odd 9,600km distance between them, Alex felt his friend's anxiety. He had always admired Sam's ability to see all points of view (Matt described it as getting the "teeny stitches right to make big tapestries"). But today, listening to Sam, Alex felt he was only being let into part of a much bigger picture, made from threads far more intricate than they first appeared.

"I've got a slogan for the branded lottery thing," he offered as an icebreaker. "If at first you don't succeed, buy, buy, buy again.'"

"Don't give up your day job, Alex," Sam replied with a frown. "... How about a slogan for a branded health service lottery: 'If at first you don't get cured, buy, buy, die or get two burgers for the price of one'."

"As the late, great Lesley Crowther would have said, 'That price, my friend, is wrong'," replied Alex. "... I'll stick with my version: a touch snappier."

"Lesley Crowther! Now that really is showing your age!" Sam said.

They chuckled. (Alex reconsidered the comedy circuit career option.)

"Look, I'll catch up with Martin, then check-in with the rest of the C-group in Latin America and so on," Sam continued.

Filling his cheeks with air like a balloon, Sam held his breath for two seconds before blowing it all away.

"Who knows, someway this might even work to our advantage," he concluded.

"It will. I'm sure," responded Alex.

There was a pause.

"Want to chat about anything else whilst we're on? Admin issues?"

"Normal service resumed," Sam noted. "OK, actually there's a couple of issues that need tidying and, thinking about it, tightening up…"

By the time the video chat ended, the sun, retiring between the skyscrapers behind Alex's desk, blinked its farewell beams of daylight.

The link was broken. Alex was gone. Sam searched his iPad's index of CEOs. Before he got to 'R', he spotted a familiar name. He remembered how Steve once had the cheeky chutzpah to offer the man product advice.

Sam smiled. From his window, the sun had barely passed its highest peak.

PART ◆ FOUR

בשלה

WHEN HE LET GO

Chapter 1

HOME WAS THE BEST place in the world.

It had all that a plump man wearing britches and carrying his cute, sensitive pet dog could need. Whenever a tree was cut down in its prime, the dog howled. Most days, the man and his pet foraged for massive boulders in the local woods. A simple life. He joyfully carried the mammoth stones with ease, from one spot to another. Best of all, the dense wood was home to wild boar which, when spit-roasted, tasted like bliss.

His community was self-sufficient. Everyone supported each other. As with many small communities, it had its own distinctive characters. The village was ruled by a kindly chief who never cared about tomorrow. Then there was the bard who stood alone in his conviction that his creativity and voice were nothing short of magnificent. A short but shrewd warrior protected the village. Village friendships kept the little fella happy and healthy (especially his camaraderie with the man in the big britches). The short warrior's super-strength came from drinking a magical potion, cooked up by the local druid. As a child, the man in the britches had fallen into a vat of the potion. (This explained his amazing strength to carry the stones.)

The village was the last small enclave in a world ruled by a hedonistic Roman empire, commanded by a conceited Caesar. However many armies were sent to 'civilise' the community, all were seen off by the man in the britches – Obelix – and his warrior friend, Asterix. The armies were little more than flies.

Even as a grown man, Sam adored the comic adventures of Asterix and Obelix, by Goscinny and Uderzo. Amongst the brilliant sagas, he treasured one story the most: *Obelix and Co*. It was kept in the office, on his SMA bookshelf, neatly stored between the Batman and Superman collection.

Obelix and Co told of how once again, Caesar was looking to defeat the seemingly unconquerable villagers.

Caesar holds a meeting in Rome with his inner cabinet of advisors. One suggests that, in order to master the village, rather than using steel-tipped swords, something far stronger was needed. If he could persuade the villagers to become addicted to money, their fighting spirit, along with social welfare concerns, would collapse.

Having tried just about everything else, and not being short of storehouses full of antoniniani, *Caesar agrees and sends the advisor as an envoy to the village.*

The advisor convinces Obelix that the useless gigantic boulders (called menhirs) *are highly valued by the empire. So much so, he is prepared to buy all the* menhirs *Obelix could gather. In return, Obelix (and Co) would be richly rewarded. Money would make him the most respected person in the community.*

At first, Obelix easily fulfils the orders. Before long, he is asked to double, then triple, the menhir *deliveries. So Obelix pays his fellow villagers to help, explaining that the harder they work, the more they will earn… and the greater the respect they'll gain from the community. At last, they would all be able to afford the finest products and services from the world beyond the village gates.*

Thanks to his newly-made wealth, Obelix changes his britches for a more elegant pair, complete with a splendid bow in primrose yellow and acorn brown. The villagers become increasingly competitive. Without money, they'd lose their dignity and the chance to own everything they could ever wish for.

The villagers grow jealous of each other. Keenness grows into enmity. Disputes erupt over the smallest trivialities. Meanwhile, Caesar is overwhelmed with piles of menhirs. His storehouses of antoniniani are totally depleted.

To avoid bankruptcy, he is forced to sell the useless boulders to his own people. An advertising campaign is launched. Slowly, the citizens start buying the menhirs. The more they buy, the higher the price for menhirs. The citizens become convinced that life without the boulders is not worth living.

Before long, the entire capital is caught up in the drive to own the massive stones, which have no function, other than to literally get in the way of even the simplest tasks, including walking down the road.

Obelix is told that there is no longer a market for his menhirs. Fights break-out in the village. "It's all his fault. What are we to do without antoniniani to buy esteem?"

The shrewd short fella, Asterix, suggest that rather than fighting each other, it would make more sense to direct their anger at the world beyond the gates. "After all, they started the whole thing."

So, fortified by drops of the druid's potion and pillars of communal strength, Obelix and company returned to the simple life of swatting away the empire's flies and enjoying all they had always owned.

Chapter 2

Wrapped around a pole, the giant Kaa scrutinised the shoppers dashing through the Southern Terrace in search of food, before darting off to complete their shopping marathon.

Sam looked through the restaurant window on the first floor of the shopping centre. Both the pole and its sculpture stood at the top of a flight of steps leading back into the heart of the mall. The serpent's body was encrusted with hundreds, if not thousands, of fake rubies. Each caught and then threw back splashes of wine-rinsed sunlight.

It suddenly struck Sam that Shepherd's Bush was an odd choice of location for the type of restaurant that had been selected. Still, it was the perfect spot to meet his lunchtime appointment.

Like so many others caught up in life's intricacies, he had postponed seeing the people who really counted, and counted on him for everything other than money.

It had been four weeks since he'd cried in front of Gerry. In the interim, Sam had attended to his usual duties at work, including a meeting with Kerry who, having returned empty handed from a potential new piece of business in Canada, decided to overlook her economy-class ticket. Also, in tandem with number '12', Sam arranged an exclusive joint interview for Nancy.

More pressing to both Ben and Matt, the latter of whom had

taken the upcoming Zeus launch under his wing, was the Asian threat to Brand Fish. Sam held face-to-face, lens-to-lens and phone-to-conference system briefings with C-levels throughout the group.

Despite everything else going on, Sam had promised himself to make time for other moments: mornings with Mia at breakfast, early evening family dinners and late night conversations with Liz.

Another long-promised moment was about to be realised.

Wearing a plain black jacket over a white shirt and black trousers, the man plucked a pistachio nut from his left pocket, and waved 'hello' to Sam with the other. The kippah on his head said the rest.

His Gibraltarian parents named him 'Mesod', which back in the day was a popular boy's name used in nearby Tangiers.

Since leaving Gibraltar, few recognised, let alone knew, his actual name.

Sam just called him 'Uncle Maurice'.

To those who didn't know him as Sam did, given Maurice's build, posture, slightly thinning hairline, broad shoulders and standing a good 1.7 metres tall, they would naturally assume he was in his late fifties.

In truth, Maurice was three score years and fifteen. To Sam, he would always be ageless.

AFTER THE RITUAL OF 'greet, seat and eat', Sam tore apart one of the three complimentary slices of sun-dried tomato and olive bread. It sat on a plate besides a stack of pencil-wide grissini.

"It's been too long, Uncle. At least a year," Sam said, before scooping a mouthful of the 'soup of the day'.

Maurice finished his silent blessing for the bread and soup, then dunked a chunk. It sliced through the melted cheese and into the brew.

"Mmm lovely… you're right, too long. So, tell me, what have you been up to? How are Elizabeth and Mia?"

"Fine. We are all doing just fine," Sam lied.

As Maurice bought another spoonful to his lips, he cast a glance at Sam: more than enough time to study his nephew's face. The smile wasn't right. The eyes weren't lively. Sam had troubles.

"I hear that you've gone into the fishmonger business," he said.

"Fishmonger? Ah, 'Brand Fish'. What do you think?"

"From what I understand about these things, it's a wonderful idea. Give a man a fish… and that kind of thing. Are you happy with it?"

"It's been difficult. But I think it may work."

"May work? Business OK?"

"You know how it is in commerce: you get a good idea, then everyone starts doing the same. Trouble is, the more others join in, the more distant that original good idea becomes. Nothing new. Just that this time… it's different. I'm tired."

Maurice could see Sam wasn't just worn out: he also seemed worn down.

"'Different' you say," Maurice registered as he placed his spoon in the emptied bowl.

Seeing the first course was done, a waitress set about fixing the table for the next.

The Denis fish (gilt-head bream) was freshly imported from Israel. It looked magnificent. Including the side orders, the meal was an ample banquet.

"Do you want to be 'mother'?" Maurice asked, offering Sam a fish knife.

"Thanks, but you do the honours. Although, maybe you'd prefer 'uncle', rather than 'mother'."

Maurice laughed. Whilst he prepared the fish, Sam munched a grissini.

"You feel that this project is becoming – as you put it, 'distant'?" Maurice continued, dividing the portions.

"Maybe it's just me and the way things just are these days. I wanted to do something right. Anyhow, it's not just the project that's getting to me."

The restaurant manager approached their table. "How are you gentlemen finding the Denis fish?" He asked politely.

"Faultless – cooked to perfection," replied Sam.

"Enjoy," answered the manager, before darting after the waitress, who was in trouble with the credit card 'touch and go' system – again.

"What's good for you, Elizabeth and Mia, Sam?" Maurice asked.

"Peace of mind," Sam answered, without a second thought.

Maurice plucked a Kalamata olive from the side salad.

"How are the headaches these days?"

"If you mean the brain, rather than the business variety... There a fewer 'auras', as my doctor calls them. She's put me on a different prescription. The throbs still throb. It's the dreams I really hate. They're weird. I'm always in some dead-end place – nowhere to turn, no escape. It's like I've run the distance, but forgot where I started, where I am, or even why I needed to get there in the first place. It's like the throbbing head: there's this pressure. Sometimes I'm trapped in immense heat, other times, cold. Always a persistent growling... barking... creeps up on me. I can never shake it lose... I wake up in sweats..."

As the words spilt, Sam was actually sweating. "Sorry, I don't why I told you all of that."

For a second time, Maurice studied his nephew's face. "Dreams, choices… it's never clear. Never has been. You've got to be careful which dreams you choose to believe in."

Maurice glanced out of the window at the shoppers, still chasing wise buys – unaware of the splashes of wine-rinsed rays that thumbed over their bodies.

"You don't need an old man to tell you that the world can be a nightmare – full of men on high horses with little regard for anyone else. You've seen it. You're a smart businessman – not to mention a dad to Mia and a husband to Liz."

Sam began to feel less vulnerable for talking about the dreams.

Maurice continued, "When I was young, and your mother was still enjoying her teen years, my school teacher encouraged the pupils to have pen pals. I was linked up with a boy from America: Francis Naphtali Fiszer."

Maurice smiled. "Frank signed his letters: 'Kind hearts are more than coronets…' (that brings back memories). Anyway, at the time Frank wasn't sure which career direction to eventually pursue. (At least that's what he allowed himself to think, but not what he actually felt: not what he wrote about, between the lines in those letters.) The the boy grew up to be a truly great man. A one-of-the-kind. A mentor. He taught people that they too were one-of-a-kind. It's just that they didn't recognise what that meant, and could mean – not just to themselves, but for everyone else."

The waitress returned.

"Desserts?" she asked.

"It's really been lovely, but we have to dash, thank you," Maurice answered.

Sam was slightly miffed. He wanted more time with his uncle.

Returning with the 'touch and go' in hand, the clearly nervous waitress typed and swiped.

Sam detected a bead of sweat on her brow. However, this time the machine 'played nice' and rewarded her with a beep, green light and till receipt.

"Fancy a coffee?" Maurice asked. "I could do with the walk. I get fidgety staying in one place too long."

"For sure," Sam answered, pleased to grab every moment.

Chapter 3

With his eyes screwed up and lips tightly sealed, Sir James peered with supercilious contempt at the shoppers who scrutinised intricate pieces of jewellery beneath glass-topped cases.

I don't want to live like you, talk like you or look like you. I'm going to be like me – Read the in-store poster featuring the former *Beathunger* star endorsing a prestigious watch brand.

How things change, Sam thought, remembering taking his fiancé (the daughter of his first business sponsor) to the globally televised 1980s *Beathunger* concert. Everyone was there, even the man who set the Sixties rock stone rolling: Bob Dylan.

Sam remembered Sir James' (back then simply called Jim) very icy, famous petition for donations: "Please, please, give money. If rock can get off its arse, you can dig into your backside pockets."

Spotting the poster, Maurice tapped his watch. "I prefer my old Timex. Still reliable, after all these years."

As they walked away from the store, an elderly gentleman led his teenage granddaughter to admire the treasures within. By the time Sam and Maurice were halfway to one of the centre's Wi-Fi connected coffee shops, the granddaughter was gazing at the picture of Sir James.

"Blimey!" she exclaimed, turning to her Bapa. "This bling must be pretty good if old-school royals like him wear it."

"Pretty damn good," the gentleman replied, admiring how a white-gloved shop assistant cradled the dazzling timepiece.

Finally, at the café, Sam managed to find a free table next to the window. Maurice took a sip of tea (no milk) from one of the café's corrugated cups. Sam supped his cappuccino.

"This is nice," Maurice said, still sipping as both he and Sam watched the shoppers through the window.

One shopper was pulling a reluctant young child towards a department store. Sam felt for the boy. (Maybe he'd heard that the store housed a cellblock of fitting rooms?)

Near the elevators, a woman was talking to a man. Clearly listening to his phone, rather than the woman, he robotically nodded to everything she said. A giggle of girls stood outside a cosmetics store. Wires leading to earphone splitters conjoined their ears. Chewing gum, the girls jutted their chins to the music.

"People think that details are in the fine print alone," Maurice said after taking a mouthful of tea.

"What do you mean?" Sam asked.

"Some spend their entire lives studying details. The likes of academics, scientists... even rabbis, mullahs, priests, gurus... Most people leave it to them to explain what's between the lines. (That's if they even care.) It's good, but it's only one way to understand."

"Sorry," chortled Sam. "It's me that doesn't understand you!"

Affably joining Sam's uneasy chuckle, Maurice took another sip.

"We all get tangled up in our lives and responsibilities. Everyone eventually comes up for air. By then, most are convinced that they're too old, too tired, too involved, seen too much, experienced too little... to have answers. 'It is what it is', they tell themselves before giving up – diving back in and getting on with their own bits and bobs. They may not like what 'it is' but it's life. The funny thing is, to find answers all they ever had to do was look. You don't need to spell 'tsuris' to see what's already in front of your eyes. Everything and everyone carries a combination key."

"Tsuris?" asked Sam.

"Don't worry about it. Just something Nat used to write in his letters."

A man sitting just a few metres beyond the café's window pulled his tuna and mayo sandwiches from a recycled brown paper bag printed with the café's logo. Taking a bite, he picked up his tablet to catch up with the daily headlines.

"Can I tell you an interesting story?" Maurice continued.

Opening his palm, Sam motioned his uncle to lead the way.

"As you know, I am a religious man. Most people think that to become religious you need to learn the ropes (so to speak) from a person steeped in things spiritual; someone who would have studied a sage and so on."

Maurice chuckled, "If only it were that easy. Knowledge shines the way to heaven. Before you can study any answers, you need to experience, see, hear… something that makes you question in the first place. If not, well, no matter how clever an answer may be, or how wise the sage, boss, leader, academic, politician… the question will never occur to you."

Sam smiled.

Taking another sip of tea, Maurice continued. "You of course know the story of Moses…"

Bible stories? Sam wondered if his uncle was getting too old. Perhaps he still somehow saw Sam as a child? He decided to go along with it. Besides, it bought back fond memories.

"Now, you'd think that the Bible would say that such a leader would have been bought up in a house of religious learning, his parents showing him the right and perfect way... In fact, the Bible explains that the truth of his upbringing couldn't be any further from being pious.

"... A dreadful dynasty was set on wiping out a fast-growing population that it considered as undesirable immigrants. Something had to be done. The king (Pharaoh) of the dynasty instructed midwives to kill all 'foreign' baby boys. However, he spared immigrants' daughters. After his birth, Moses' mother couldn't keep her baby a secret for long. So she placed him inside a waterproofed basket, which she set adrift on the River Nile. A little crazy don't you think?" Maurice asked Sam, who, despite himself, was rather enjoying the story.

Maurice continued: "From the banks of the river his older sister Miriam followed the basket. Eventually, none other than the Pharaoh's daughter, who was bathing in the Nile, found him. Now, the Egyptian Nile deity, Hapi, was considered the god of fertility. Without Hapi, Egypt would have perished. (The Egyptians often revered Hapi even above Ra, the sun god.)"

Maurice paused for effect.

"... Convinced the child was a divine gift from Hapi, Pharaoh's daughter adopted him. As you can imagine, it was all kept very 'hush-hush'. Her maidservants were instructed to care privately for Moses until he was a grown lad. At that point, Pharaoh's daughter introduced Moses to the king. Given Moses' supposed lineage, Pharaoh took a shine to the kid. In fact, some say the lad was called 'Moses' from the root 'M-S-S'. In the ancient Egyptian language it means 'son of', like 'Ramses' means 'son of the god Ra'. Others say it means 'take out', because Moses was taken out of the river...."

Unsure where Maurice was actually heading with all of this, Sam listened on.

"Moses grew up in the Pharaoh's palace. This fortress hosted parties with the most exotic wine, women, food and debauchery that Cecil B. de Mille's Hollywood could ever imagine. While Pharaoh's dynastic seal was stamped on everything that could be traded, the king was not exactly the first name that would come to mind as moral parent of the year."

Sam laughed. He was a kid again. The story was never told like this when he was at school. His uncle was definitely in the wrong business.

"The day arrives for Moses to pay the foreigners a visit. Despite his celebrity lifestyle – a million miles away from the immigrants' reality – somehow Moses instinctively felt a bond.

"On the way, he comes across a beefy Egyptian yob. The hooligan decides to beat one of the foreigners to a pulp. (Who knows, maybe he wanted the adrenalin rush?) Incensed by all this, Moses looks this way and that, and finding there was no man around, he beat up the Egyptian, not just to a pulp, but to death! He then buried him.

"So now Moses is right in the middle of a crime scene. What with his connections and status, Moses needn't have worried about the yob. In fact, no one would have cared. Do you see, Sam?"

Sam had lost the plot. "Sorry, see what?"

Finishing the tea, Maurice explained.

"Here's a man caught between two worlds. His world was all about fine arts, streamlined chariots, big names, culture – the whole Academy Awards night treatment. But... his heart was in a totally different place. 'He looked this way and that'; Moses reached a decisive crossroad. As long as he remained uncertain of which road to take, he realised that as a person, 'there was no man'. Moses would always be trapped between what he had, and who he was – and meant to become."

Stepping out of his childhood shadows, Sam put down his cappuccino. A familiar prickle crept up his hand. This time, rather than just stab, each tingle felt soothing.

Somehow Sam knew it had nothing whatsoever to do with the coffee beans.

Chapter 4

"SCHOOL'S OUT FOREVER...!" SAM sung as Mia stepped into the XK.

She was delighted. No more exams, plus a suddenly announced holiday just around the corner. Things were cool.

"You think you did well?" Sam asked.

"As best as I could."

"That's good enough for me."

The car stopped at a zebra crossing. Mia watched as a mother with a wriggling child struggled across.

Once clear, Sam drove on.

"Anyway, how come you're picking me up?" asked Mia.

"What, you think I wouldn't be here on a day like this?"

Mia was delighted.

With an eye on the Satnav, Sam headed towards home.

"So where are we going?" asked Mia.

"To pick up Mum. I was thinking about treating you both to a meal at The Broadway in the village."

Mia smiled. Even with thoughts of sea and sand, waist-watching could be put on hold – at least, for tonight. Her family was together.

"Do you fancy grabbing something for the holiday? We could head into town," Sam suggested.

Mia considered the offer for all of three seconds, finally deciding that the prospect of being with Mum and Dad, doing whatever, far outweighed another Voi top, or a pair of Miss Sixty jeans.

"Music time," Sam announced.

"I left my player at home," answered Mia.

"No problem. Let's go classic," Sam countered, selecting BBC Radio 2 from the on-screen system.

DJ Simon Mayo came on. *"… Another sweet answer, I think. Speaking of which, before the news, here's a delicious number from Mr Mathis. Ah memories… Noel Edmonds, Jim'll Fix It, Top of the Pops…"*

The Bowers & Wilkins' diaphragms resonated to the opening orchestral chords of 'I'm Stone Love in Love with You'. Steering the car into a clear highway, Sam turned up the volume.

If I were a businessman, I'd sit behind a desk.
I'd be so successful, I would scare Wall Street to death.
I would hold a meeting for the Press to let them know,
I did it all, coz I'm stone in love with you.

"Now *that's* a tune. It's right up there with Herman's Hermits."

Mia knew the Hermits. One of their songs was Dad's ringtone for Mum.

"When I dated Mum we used to go to this place in North London, ending up there for a snack after a club…"

"… My Dad, the disco-king," Mia said wryly.

"I think that might be stretching it a touch. Mind you, I'll have you know, your mother was quite a dancer. Still is. As for me, well I could have taught The King of Pop a thing or two." Sam said. "… Still could."

"That wouldn't be difficult," Mia ribbed, "he's dead."

"Good point."

Mia laughed.

"Hey, it wasn't just clubs," Sam continued, feeling uncomfortable about the gag. "… There were movies, concerts and friends… Somehow, more often than not, we ended up at that place in Camden. The food was simple but OK. The owner must have only owned around twenty songs on his machine… I remember Cher, Babylon Zoo, George Michael, Michael Jackson, of course… and that one by Johnny M. Thinking about it, the restaurant's music playlist was as short as their choice of omelettes (plain or with processed cheese). It repeated itself in the same way, too."

Mia giggled again, Sam joined in. (Still smiling, Mia made a mental note to 'iTunes' Babylon Zoo, and maybe even the Mathis number. Mum would like it.)

The XK hummed softly as it carried its passengers towards the house. Sam turned down the radio to a comfortable backdrop of unchained melodies. Mia listened to her father's tales about rain-drenched first meetings, adventures with friends and ice creams on the beach.

By the time they reached home, trees, streetlights, bikers beating deadlines, cabbies with VIP airport fares… had all passed by Mia's window. Time seemed to go in a flash. She was engrossed in the stories. Each was filled with Dad's smiles and Mum's fortitude. Mia felt as contented as a chirpy cockney tucking into a Holy Ghost and Clothes Pegs sarnie.

Chapter 5

Punctiliously following Zeus' lightning bolt design, Dan smoothed the left edge of each logo down to a smidgen under 100cm wide. The right tips were narrowed down to 28cm. Both stood bang on 1000cm tall and a stroke over 11cm deep. Each of the two thunderbolts had a subtle silky gleam.

Once machined and shaped, Dan bored holes, each just under 8cm in diameter, into the ends. The sections were scrupulously levelled and sanded. Dan swept away the dead skins of dust from each naked hunk of wood. Carefully troweling, he filling in the planks' open pores. Then, returning from a coffee in the café, waited for the process to heal.

Wood-sealed, fine layers of boiled linseed oil were rubbed into the grain. The wood appeared as if it was bleeding oil. After two hours, Dan massaged more linseed into the now stunning wings of wood. With the outside light from his window fading, Dan adjusted the studio lights to full, before repeating the application.

He took the precaution of submerging the rags in a bucket of water. Apart from being laborious, the boiled linseed oil made the job dangerous. The oil-soaked rags could cause the lightning bolts to spontaneously combust.

On the fourth day, Dan glued fine strips of metal, each measuring

5.08cm wide and just 0.04cm deep, around the entire outer edge of both logos. The division added to the impression of movement. From a distance the logos were identical. However, close up, each one's grain thumbprint told a different story.

Dan allowed one more day to pass: five days altogether.

On the sixth day, a Monday (27 days since selecting the red oak), Dan dipped into a bag of dried fruit and nuts and looked at the work. Very good, he thought.

Chapter 6

"I t's the least I could do… I'm sure it… and he… will be adored by the critics. Anyway, one way or the other, I'll see you." (The voice at the other end laughed.)

"Take care buddy."

With that, Sam pressed the button and ended the call.

"I'm sorry," Sam said, studying her face. It was beautiful. "In fact…" Sam continued and turned the phone completely off.

Used to waiting, she smiled forlornly.

"I think… actually I know, I'm a lucky man," Sam whispered. "I am also a dumb one. I've thrown away too much time."

She touched his lips gently.

Lifting her right hand, she curled, then presented her little finger. He opened his left hand, letting his own finger curl over with hers. Finally, each fully held fast to the other's hand.

They comforted each other: explaining, reassuring, acknowledging… in every minutiae of detail. But nothing was said.

In the distance a dog yapped. Sam didn't notice.

Chapter 7

DR KEITH ANTHONY VINCENT (MD) was thankful for the swivel seat cum six-foot six-inch flat bed. He slept right through most of the flight's 10 hours and 15 minutes. After a month of congresses, meetings and conferences, he deserved it.

The original plan was to take a short break with the family, then get back to the theatre. But when his PA, Dana, mentioned Geraldine's name, he accepted the call. Her name took him back to the Keck days. Tony had just graduated. At the time he was in London to experience a genuine royal wedding.

Lining the royal procession route, Geraldine, an exquisite British rose, had asked if he "wouldn't mind budging up a bit". Along with thousands of others, they had set up a makeshift camp the day before. Twenty-four hours of chitchatting, sharing food, being in the bosom of flag-waving Brits, and most of all, discovering that they had both just completed medical degrees, guaranteed a long-term friendship.

… This case involved someone she considered as a dear friend and she was worried. The cues were more than enough for Tony to accept the invitation. (After, of course, he had finished the talks).

Tony reasoned with himself that it had been a while since he had been in London. Once business was done, he might even fly Janet (his wife) over for a week. The budget more than covered it. He could always get Dana to upgrade the executive suite at the Canary Wharf Marriott.

Since the original call, Dana had arranged for Tony to meet up with her friend, a fella called Sam. Google had lots on him. The guy was big in advertising and the media. Sam was due to talk at the O2 Arena. Dana emailed the information to Tony.

Spotting on the web that the Marriott was conveniently close to the venue, and that the airline was part of a global airline alliance, it was a no-brainer decision. Dana made sure Tony's Club Advance card was suitably topped up. He had three hotel cards. She always tried to stick to using just two of them. (Tony was going for maximum points: a treat for Janet and the kids.) The Marriott was one favourite, the Hilton the other.

Tony had read about the Zeus launch. It was all over the web. The first global TV commercial – live.

Typical of the Brits, Tony thought, as he watched the River Thames curve around the white crested arena. He remembered it from the Olympics' basketball games, which hosted coach Mike Krzyzewski's dream team. Before long, he was looking at the Houses of Parliament. They always go large and in style, Tony smiled to himself. But he also felt irked that he had missed the Queen's Diamond Jubilee pageant.

Adjusting the aircraft's speed and positioning, the flight's captain checked the panels for the initial approach fix (IAF). The stewardess checked Tony's seat buckle.

It would be good to see Geraldine. Besides, from what Tony had read, the event looked like it would give his ventromedial prefrontal cortex a rest from ethics surrounding metastatic carcinomas, intracranial metastases and stereotactic radiotherapy…

Chapter 8

Ten thousand people fantasised of becoming the next Beckham, Woods, Shakes-Drayton, Bryant, Blair, Rooney, Williams, Ronaldo... The O2 Arena could have easily accommodated 20,000. Nevertheless, thanks to clever backstage draping, the venue looked full.

Amy stood by one of the stage entrances looking at the enthralled audience. They had just watched Daniel Levy, tennis coach to Hollywood's elite, recommending Zeus equipment and clothing. Amy could see why he was so popular. The athletic coach was tall, handsome, smart and, as a speaker, very relaxed, not to mention extremely funny.

All in all, the project had progressed to plan, right down to Pete convincing the T-shirt people to supply one Ecocreeper shirt per ticket – with a cut off date of 12 days before the event. Including an extra 500 garments held in reserve, Pete's tactics had hit the mark.

The TV stations co-operated as if they were first cousins. Matt wasn't surprised. The event build-up had sent Zeus' competitors into TV space overdrive. However, Barnes and Roberts' international media buying teams had already tied the channels into securing the top slots for Zeus. The deals included sponsoring online catch-ups, as well as tablet 'watch, chat 'n' swipe' packages.

Small Fry's video intro was a hit. The story took place some 30 years in the future. Its voice-over featured an elderly man. He recalled how as kids he and his friends were too poor to afford tickets for the Olympic Games. Instead they held their own mini Olympics.

The kids drew chalked racetrack lines on local side roads that stood below a cityscape dominated by the O2. High jumps were cobbled together with broom handles, scraps of scaffolding and a mattress nicked from the local junkyard. Football simply required boxes drawn on the walls of the local park. The man cracked a joke that everyone agreed to leave out swimming from the games. Shooting, as always, would continue – mainly from the next postcode from their Manor.

Towards the film's end, the man (now revealed as his own age) stood outside an ultra-modern stadium in his Zeus trainers. His weathered hands held a gold Olympics medal. The camera angle turned around and then away from the man. It panned out wide and high, showing his half-lit silhouette alongside a group of others.

Some held tablets, another a briefcase, others, medals. One carried a mop. Set against a stunning sunrise, the magnificent illuminated stadium overshadowed them all. Finally, as the light rose over London's River Jordan, a discreet Zeus thunderbolt with its slogan, *You will because you can*, faded into the centre of the closing scene.

Matt had made sure that the video could be edited down to no less than four different TV commercial and YouTube lengths.

Everything was perfect, including, thanks to Cliff, the PR timing. He made sure the event was held on a Thursday (ideal for the press, who were promised 'follow-up weekend specials'). It also meant that the gig was held too late in the week for any brand competitors to steal the limelight.

Chapter 9

Precision, especially at events, came at a price: hard work and judicious use of gaffer tape.

Two days earlier, the arena was a chaotic conundrum of cameras, jumper cables, video systems, lasers, mirrors, broadcast engineers, smoke machines, set designers, cups of tea, mixing desks, projectors, pulleys, lights and frantic rabbits, tested to their limits by twitchy managers. Luckily, Amy had planned ample time for crews to get rigged, rehearsals to be made and definitive details double-checked.

Despite her last minute nerves, Matt assured Amy that Sam would be fine without formal rehearsals. "He's a professional's professional."

Huw had written the script. It received both his own and Sam's sign-off. Amy accepted Matt's promises, albeit guardedly.

She needn't have worried, Sam had already phoned George from Zeus. He was up to speed.

"No problem," George had told Sam, adding, "… by the way, Kris is really excited about being included in the new Tate exhibition…"

Amy's Wednesday schedule included a 10 a.m. delivery of the logos. A production assistant was instructed to book a lorry that was big enough to store them, as well as three additional deliverymen beefy enough to carry the load.

The lorry arrived at 10.30. Overseeing the haulage team, Dan started to help unload the cargo. In situ, the logos were bigger than Amy had imagined them to be on paper, or could appreciate back in the workshop. (She was pleased that she had budgeted for the extra hands.)

Once the logos were positioned on the arena floor, Dan was greeted by the project's stage manager who, following her training at LAMDA (London Academy of Music and Dramatic Art), carefully watched Dan guide an unseen rigger lowering down two lines of galvanised cable, each connected to a springhook.

High over the arena, the rigging's reinforced steel gridiron ceiling stretched all the way from one end of the building to the other. The grid supported a 'fly system' of headblock mounts, which carried counterweights (known as 'arbours'), pulleys and cables.

The mounts' coordinates were marked by 'fix points' that ran along the reinforced matrix (itself marked by 60 master sections). Anything from scenery (known in the business as 'drops') to a flying giant toy soldier (from a performance of *The Nutcracker*) and creatures from outer space (Jeff Wayne's *The War of the Worlds*) could be suspended and rolled along a track, as according to the strict instructions of an often highly strung set designer.

The gridiron's architectural engineer – a man called Simon Hanford – had always been both practical as well as smart. Rather than going from a classroom straight onto the drawing board, his career actually started trussed up in a harness. Back then, he was an apprentice rigger who worked for a self-employed Head Flyman. (At the time, the job was the closest Simon could get to what was to become a lifelong passion for orienteering.)

Having seen how things worked in practice, Simon decided to learn why they worked in theory. He studied civil engineering. Drawing on his experience as a young rigger, beyond grasping the mechanics of tensile structures alone, Simon understood that any Head Flyman trussed up in the grid should be able to follow a set director's instructions.

To cover everyone, his grid blueprint took into consideration both 'right' and 'left' brain biased riggers, stage managers and, of course, set designers. That way, the Head Flyman in particular, would be given the best chance to get into a set designer's good books.

Simon assigned every mount's 'fix point' with a classification number between one and thirty. For extra assurance he gave each of the grid's 60 master sections its own number, together with a name (which Simon slyly named after mountains).

So, for example, '1/Everest' would be the master section row at the extreme end of the back of the house (over seating blocks 411/412); '15:1/Everest' pinpointed the mount in the middle of that particular master section's row; '60/Olympus' was the master section row above the other end of the arena (behind the stage, covering block 115/116); while '15:60/Olympus' was that master section's middle fix point.

Simon named the centre master row '30/Fuji'. Therefore, '15:30/Fuji' would be right in the middle of the auditorium.

Dan, who had just scooped some grease onto his finger, would have easily understood the system. However, busy swivelling his finger inside each aperture at either end of the first 10-metre logo, for today at least, it all went over his head.

Dan secured and shackled the black cables through their freshly anointed gaps, and onto springhooks. He then gave the 'thumbs-up' signal to the man in the rigging. Slowly the cables took up the slack. The first logo rose. The hoist's track wheels gently moved the logo towards the backstage area, coming to a final rest behind the stage.

Facing the main arena, its centre was near 15:60/Olympus.

Once confident that the first logo was steady, Dan turned towards the stage manager, who remained standing besides the second logo. The stage manager gave Dan the 'thumbs up'. In turn, Dan did the same for the man in the rigging.

Waiting for Dan to return to where the stage manager was now busying himself with a clipboard of notes, the man in the rigging took a slurp of tea from his flask. Around the time he was considering taking a biscuit from a twin-pack bought that morning at his regular café in Haddo Street, he heard Dan calling.

"OK. She's all fastened!" Dan shouted, having shackled the second logo to its springhooks.

Watching, the stage manager looked curiously at Dan. He wondered why Dan didn't use a walkie-talkie.

The man in the rigging pressed buttons and pulled levers. Gradually, the second logo began to lift.

Wheels rolled the logo towards 'fix point' 32:49 (between 'Nebo' and 'Peale').

The logo (now as high as its brother) was turned. The tip of its left end dipped towards the centre stage area.

Once again, Dan waved a 'thumbs up'.

The rigger crosschecked the grid-plan against his set of written instructions, which lay in front of the still unopened packet of biscuits. Then, using his walkie-talkie, the stage manager confirmed some adjustments.

The cable attached to the second logo's larger base (its right end facing the auditorium area) was hoisted up a further 56°. The final tilt created the impression that the thunderbolt was striking directly from the sky.

Dan gave the rigger another 'thumbs up'.

The stage manager was pleased.

The effect was dramatic. The fine silver edges gave a finishing touch to the sense of lightning. Once some strategically positioned spots were added, it would all look spectacular.

Chapter 10

LIZ WONDERED WHAT OTHER secrets the good doctor had been hiding all these years. She was sat next to Gerry, who was beside a charming man called Tony. He had flown in the day before from America. In addition to being charismatic, Dr Keith Anthony Vincent MD might just save Sam's life.

Sixteen hours earlier, as the hotel's Golden Keys accredited concierge ordered Tony a taxi to Montagu Square, Liz had been packing bags ready to be loaded into the Porsche. Mia was still deciding between the red or blue top.

Even that very morning, at the last minute, Mia changed her plans to join her mother at the actual event. Instead, she wanted to get hold of a Hollister dress that would go perfectly with either the red or blue. (But she packed both.)

Mia promised her mother to catch the live commercial on her iPad. Most teens would have considered the line-up as irresistible; but Mia had grown accustomed to her father's 'showbiz' environment. She arranged to meet the family after the show, by the O2 fountains. From there, they would head to London City Airport.

After a duty-free drink or two, flight and nap, the family would join the 566,500 people who each day walked past Times Square's digital billboards at the corner of the world.

Chapter 11

M ATT LOOKED STRAIGHT INTO Sam's eyes. "Ready?"

"As ever."

"Did you like what I did with Huw's script?" Matt asked.

"Nice touch," replied Sam, smiling at his friend, who would always need that little bit of fuss. (Sam knew if ever he needed encouragement, it would be returned with interest.)

As Matt studied the amendments one more time, Sam noticed a young man with thick, wavy hair. The man was stealing an innocent peep at Amy's smartly suited backside. Judging by her knowing playful response, and the man's backstage pass, Sam assumed they were close.

Over on the stage, Ben Bueno and the band were tuned up and set to perform their specially composed song, 'Be Someone'. Thanks to Keith Bishop (the band's sharp-minded manager who mentioned their Brits potential to those who could make a difference) the band could expect to earn a tidy little sum from the track.

Combining forces with CPC and Katherine Moon (a tenaciously talented producer) Keith arranged for the group to join Elbow as judges on a new reality show, *Victorious Voices*. (Whilst Ben had composed the Zeus theme, Elbow had penned the BBC's Olympic tune.)

"We've come a long way you and I," Sam said, turning to Matt. "… kitchens to commercials: global at that."

"As Karen 'C' put it, 'we've only just begun…'," Matt replied.

Sam cringed playfully.

Matt shrugged his shoulders.

"Times change, priorities change," Sam confessed, nodding to a rack of TV engineers coordinating their editing suite sliders with fail-safe stopwatches.

Matt snickered. He took a second glance at Sam's eyes. There was something different there. Despite first spotting the change when Huw was suggested as scriptwriter, Matt had chosen not so much as to ignore it, but to wait until Sam was ready to talk.

Ben and the band finished singing the catchy Zeus theme:

"Open all your doors, now you know what time is for: time to make it yours…"

The audience cheered. The floor director waved at Amy.

Amy lightly placed her hand on Sam's arm. "Cue you!" she joked gently.

Matt watched as his best friend stepped into a blanket of shadow, stage left.

From John O' Groats, Scotland to Cabo San Lucas, Mexico, from TV showrooms to train platforms, people stooped over their hand-held tablets watching the Zeus logo appear. A fish swam up from the bottom of the screen.

Mia tuned in via her Air Media server, just as the caption, *Together we serve you,* appeared.

Chapter 12

A DIMINUTIVE GOLF BALL ROLLED onto the stage floor. Most didn't even notice it coming to a halt at the centre. Gradually, the ball began to throb. As if an object inside was pushing to escape, the ball wobbled and stretched one way, then the other. Finally, with a shudder, it metamorphosed into a tennis ball. The front row seats pointed out the strange phenomenon to the second row. Seven further pulses and the back row had also heard.

The tennis ball began to throb once more, until it moulded itself into a rugby ball. As with the golf ball, the rugby ball wobbled and pounded into all manner of distorted shapes until, with a final curve, it transformed into a football.

Tony was fascinated. The balls were apparently real.

Towards the back of the stage, the blue lights pointing at the first Zeus logo began to pulse. Slowly the football joined in, beating like Doctor Who's second heart to the rhythm of the other. A distant drum was heard. As the thump drew closer, it became faster.

Three narrow bright white lights were aimed at the second Zeus logo, tilted towards the stage. The spots caught the logo's silver edges. The entire piece looked like a live lightning bolt coming from above.

A crash. The football exploded. All the lights, except the spots still focused on the stage's main logo, blacked out. The audience's faces were lit by a blaze of red light. The Zeus thunderbolt turned into a furnace of terracotta red.

Where once stood a ball, a point of light pierced through a haze of smoke.

A man stepped forward.

"My name is George."

As with the different balls, to all intents and purposes, George was seemingly solid. However, like them, he was in fact a 3D apparition. A central camera slowly zoomed into his upper body.

"Zeus is an ideas factory," he announced. "My job is to ensure that everything we do, or get involved with, has intrinsic value to people.

"In addition to our products helping athletes be their best, our foundation enables people to reach their potential. We are committed to supporting the most needy: keeping them healthy, clothed, housed and educated. We – or rather – you, our customers, provide the financial kick-start to get business ideas off the ground. The work provides jobs, which feed people and keeps someone's world – our world – running forwards.

"Zeus is proud to be part of Brand Fish. The initiative reflects our commitment towards a closer global society.

"Before I explain more, I want to introduce a friend. Ladies and gentlemen, a man who I can personally promise always puts his best foot forward: Mr Sam Roberts."

Chapter 13

A SLENDER BEAM OF LIGHT reached into the shadows and picked up the red pumps' glossy Zeus logos. Next, the beam lapped his body. Finally, Sam stepped towards George's 3-D image.

Rubbing his eyes, Sam stooped to pick up a small bottle of mineral water from the stage floor. Then, making his way towards the centre stage edge, he took a gulp.

Sam spoke.

"Today there's a real chance to proliferate ideas to such an degree that everyone feels a genuine sense of achievement and purpose. Brand Fish is about partnership. Tearing down walls, bridging abilities with passions…"

… For a brief moment, Sam lost his line of thought. He took another gulp of water. What with having just seen a man appear from a 'solid' ball and now Sam's exceptionally slick yet simple arrival, the audience was mesmerised.

Turning away from camera one's scripted autocue machine, Sam took three steps forwards towards the stage's centre. The second cameraman was bemused. Quickly taking an instruction over the 'cans' to pick up the action, a third camera panned towards Sam.

Sam continued.

This time, in his own words.

"When I was a kid, my father taught me an unusual word. It was in Hebrew: 'Mehilla'. It's about forgiveness.

"Since the beginning, I have spent my entire career convincing people to have faith in brands. For some, their beliefs were realised. For others, dreams still linger. In many parts of the world, people pray for a roof over their heads. They want to feel safe, loved, respected: complete.

"The lucky ones will have at least seventy years to fulfil their goals.

"I once heard that we are the consequences of the choices that we make. Others succumb to what they are given. A few prefer not to choose anything (and that's their choice)."

The audience laughed an uncertain chuckle.

Sam continued.

"Once, nobody had to search for meanings. Everyone knew truth for what it was, rather than what people would later assume it to be.

"Things of our own making became branded with apparent, rather than actual, truth (which by then, like my cranky memory, we had totally forgotten). We were condemned to spend our short lives dreaming of meanings created from new beliefs dreamt up in our own heads."

Again the audience wasn't sure if Sam had delivered some sort of joke. Playing safe, they gave another half-hearted chuckle.

Sam grinned.

"For eternity, we served life-long sentences searching for meaning, continually encountering different possibilities of why we exist, but never finding the answer.

"So I owe you an apology. Maybe others like me do, too. That's their choice. All I can ask is for your forgiveness so that you can realise all you are, rather than forever promising to become, or assuming you will remain being. From today, together, with your permission, we can take Brand Fish to an even higher level..."

Desperately scanning through his script for Sam's lines to cue the camera back to George, an exasperated man from the TV crew looked quizzically at his colleagues.

Glancing up at the rig, Sam whispered in a small, tender voice: "Release these stars."

The second Zeus logo, tilting from the rigging above towards the stage below, creaked.

Its short cable buckled.

The remaining cable, at the thunderbolt's heavier end, crunched on the strain. The sudden jolt sent shockwaves through the wooden icon. The abrupt loss of tension caused the larger end of the logo to rock back on itself, almost touching the rigging. As it kissed the grid, the cable snarled.

The springhook snapped.

Enough momentum had been generated to hurtle the thunderbolt forwards, flying at breakneck speed towards Sam.

Ten thousand dreamers, including Liz, Matt and Mia, joined by millions more tuned in from around the world, watched in horror as the tip of the logo struck Sam's body, puncturing straight through his chest, carrying him to where he finally lay slumped, pinned vertically to the first logo at the rear of the stage.

A brown pool of blood dripped from Sam's lacerated body.

The arena fell silent: as empty as an abandoned cinema.

OMEGA

תולדת

GENERATIONS

Chapter 1

IN KEEPING WITH TRADITION, the family – Martha, Liz, Matt and Mia – each threw a handful of earth into the open grave of Samuel Yehoshua Eved Roberts. Passing a line of people stretched back as far as the cemetery's first rows of loved ones, the family slowly walked towards Hoop Lane's communal prayer room.

Behind them, each mourner in turn cast his and her own handful of earth into the grave.

A YEAR PASSED. THE INITIAL criminal investigation, which included a thorough technical debriefing, concluded that the accident couldn't be attributed to one specific person or mechanical failure. At best, despite the family's protests, the final incident report concluded that some kind of cable slippage had started a chain reaction: it was an act of God.

Chapter 2

In January, on average, the temperature could reach as high as 30° centigrade in Brazil. Thankfully for the people running in the centre of the spectacular arena, as well as for the spectators, during this particular summer it mostly hovered at around 22°.

Alex sat next to Liz and Mia.

"This is quite something," he said, taking in the atmosphere.

Pushing the 'Jackie O' Ray-Bans further up the bridge of her nose, Mia agreed.

"I'm back," Matt called, holding a disposable tray whilst weaving his way to the empty seat.

"'M' emailed. The shop is fine. Amy's got it under control."

Finally settled back into his seat, Matt passed the Starbucks' tray to Liz, who passed it further along to Mia and then Alex. The coffee was hot: certainly too hot to drink in the late morning sun. Yet Matt being Matt, insisted they all "give it a shot".

Alex slipped his cup under the seat. Turning to Liz, he said, "I guess now is as good a time as ever."

He drew an envelope from his inside jacket pocket.

"What for?" asked Liz.

"This."

Alex handed her the envelope. Liz glanced at Matt, then Mia.

Taking the envelope, she pulled out a sheet of paper and read.

"…What is it?" Mia asked.

Liz didn't answer.

"If I may…" Alex suggested.

Liz nodded in assent.

"It," Alex continued, "is something that some time ago your dad told me to draw up. At the time, I questioned the whole thing. In fact, I even tried to warn him against it. Your father was a very stubborn man."

Matt smiled. Alex had already told him about the contents of the envelope two days earlier. Respecting Sam's wishes and keeping to Alex's strict instructions, Matt hadn't mentioned a word to either Liz or Mia.

Liz rested the sheet on her lap. Picking up her coffee, she stared at a whisper of smoke rise up from the brew.

Matt spoke.

"Around the time of the 2012 Games, Sam opened a private account. He invested everything that he earned from number 12's involvement with Brand Fish."

Alex turned to Mia.

"Your dad instructed that his entire cut earned specifically from '12' should go to people living in shanty towns. He chose seven spots around the world: places like Rocinha."

Mia was still puzzled.

Alex nodded towards a large section of the arena directly opposite from where they sat.

"One of the stipulations that he asked me to include was that, providing there was enough profit to cover the costs, a complete block in the arena of the next Olympic Games should be reserved and donated to Rocinha's local kids and elderly."

They all gazed on as the vast block of people opposite cheered an athlete who was just about to cross the finishing line.

Above the arena, 12's distinctive brand colours blended perfectly into the backdrop. The athlete won the race, breaking his personal record.

Some 14km away, towering 700 metres over favelas, beaches, homes and business districts, a 39.6 metre statue watched as endless waves of secretaries and commas of balding men scurried along towards what they hoped would turn out to be a day of semi-colons rather than a full stop.

About the Author

J ONATHAN GABAY HAS WORKED with the some of the biggest brands and their agencies.

Leading educational establishments and marketing practionners recommend his books. Titles have been translated worldwide.

Jonathan has taught literally thousands of professional marketers throughout the world. He is also a much sought after public speaker.

News outlets including: ITN, BBC, Bloomberg, CNN, Channel 4, Channel 5, ABC and many more, trust Jonathan for his insights on commercial, political, sports and entertainment business stories in the headlines.

Jonathan's websites are:
www.jonathangabay.com
www.brandforensics.co.uk

Also by Jonathan Gabay

- *Soul Traders – The Dark Side of Marketing and Propaganda:* Marshall Cavendish (editions internationally, including China) (2009)

- *Handlarze Dusz (Soul Traders* in Polish): Flashbook (2011)

- *Write Persuasive Copy*: Flash, Hatchett (2011)

- *Marketing for Success*: Flash, Hatchett (2011)

- *The Marketing Century*: CIM (2011)

- *Improve Your Copywriting*: Hodder Headline (2010)

- *Make a Difference with Your Marketing – Teach Yourself*: Hatchett (2010)

- *Gabay's Copywriters' Compendium*: Elsevier Hatchett (Three editions – 2005, 2007, 2009)

- *Teach Yourself Marketing*: Hodder Headline (Three editions – 1995, 1998, 2003)

- *Reinvent Yourself*: Momentum Books (2002)

- *Web Marketing in a Week*: Chartered Management Institute / Hodder and Stoughton (2000/02)

- *Como Te Êxito no Cibermarketing numa Semana*: Brazil Practicos de Gâstao (2000)

- *The Guru Book (3) Cool Brands*: Cool Brands (2009)

- *Reinvent Yourself* (Russian Translation): Pearson Education (2012)

- *Heroes.com: The Names and Faces Behind the Dot Com Era*: Hodder and Stoughton (2000)

- *Imaginative Marketing*: Hodder Headline (1998)

- *Teach Yourself Copywriting*: Hodder Headline (Four editions) (1996)

- *The Meaning of Life*: Virgin Books (Three editions internationally) (1995)

- *The Little Black Book*: Corgi (1985)